Emily Soldene

My Theatrical and Musical Recollections

Emily Soldene

My Theatrical and Musical Recollections

ISBN/EAN: 9783743392687

Manufactured in Europe, USA, Canada, Australia, Japa

Cover: Foto ©Thomas Meinert / pixelio.de

Manufactured and distributed by brebook publishing software (www.brebook.com)

Emily Soldene

My Theatrical and Musical Recollections

MY
THEATRICAL AND MUSICAL RECOLLECTIONS

BY

EMILY SOLDENE

AUTHOR OF "YOUNG MRS. STAPLES"

NEW EDITION

DOWNEY & CO., Limited
12, YORK STREET, COVENT GARDEN, LONDON
1898

LONDON:
PRINTED BY GILBERT AND RIVINGTON, LD,
ST. JOHN'S HOUSE, CLERKENWELL ROAD, E.C.

MY THEATRICAL AND MUSICAL RECOLLECTIONS

INTRODUCTORY.

UNDER the shadow of the Southern Cross, 13,000 miles from that bright little, tight little, island—the remembrance of which produces a lump in the throat, and spoils one's favourite effect when singing "Home, Sweet Home"—in this land within whose vast and illimitable gates stands with wide open, welcoming arms, the young, and lovely, and laughing, and robust figure of a great and mighty future; this land of silent, immeasurable, undiscovered mysteries and treasures, of wingless birds and walking fishes, of giant, feathery, fluttering ferns, of huge fruits and wonderful flowers, of everlasting light and warmth and sunshine; a land whose prodigal and riotous profusion brings forth the red and shining gold, and gleaming, glittering gems; a land where nature soothes, and you dream dreams, fairy dreams, and realise them, too, sometimes—well, in this far-off land "I shut my eyes," as the Baillee in "Les Cloches de Corneville" observes, and try to call up recollections of bygone days. What a formidable undertaking! To creep back over the years that are past with soft and furtive footstep, lest the awakened and misty thoughts flee, fade away, and disappear back into the tiny and hidden chambers of the brain, to try and open the jewelled caskets of the memory; back, back to the days of childhood, when all the world was a Fairy Tale; back to the days when the spotted sea-shell on the parlour table whispered to listening baby ears of distant lands and distant delights, of surging seas and roc's eggs, of genii, and gnome; back to the days when the tangled thoughts, intricate as any spider's web, tired the childish brain, and brought the restful "Dustman" to the wondering, half-closed childish eyes; back to the days of painfully acquired, prosaic "one, two and three" syllables; back to the days, the joyous days of first heard music, when the winds to each separate tree sang a different tune; back to the veritable distractions that fell upon the ardent but stumbling student of "five lines and four spaces," the impatient inquirer into the mysteries of "Do-re-mi-fa"; back to the memories of mighty artistes, to the memories of the Grand Opera, memories that, impalpable and gauze-like, elude one, and get mixed up with the gay and festive Music Hall; back—way back— back to the days when Plancus was Consul, when we were all young; back to the birth of that gilded, glittering, tinselled glory, "The Opera

Bouffe" stage. Ah! the days when we went gipsying, a long time ago.

I don't remember when I learned to read. It seems to me I could always read. For eleven years I was an only child. My parents were conservative, and my sources of information limited, but a wilful child will have its way, and my earliest studies, in spite of supervision, were quite mixed; my personal (most of it concealed) library consisting of the Bible, several ragged volumes of Harrison Ainsworth, " Old St. Paul's," " Tower of London," &c., " The Arabian Nights," " Robinsoe Crusoe," " St. Clair of the Isles; "— how I did love Ambrosine (I remember she used to carry round her neck a little bag in which were the parings of St. Bridget's nails)—" A Casket of Literary Gems," " Rasselas, or the Happy Valley," a small " Beauties of Shakespeare," " The Pilgrim's Progress," Byron's " Don Juan," and, dreadfully shabby and covered with a bit of scrubby Scotch plaid, Gibbon's " Decline and Fall of the Roman Empire." All these books, except the Bible, were read with much difficulty and danger, and in defiance of maternal prohibition of the most pronounced and severe description, fiction of any kind being *ex purgatoris* and regarded as the work of the Devil. Naturally, being cut off from the legitimate enjoyment of these interesting and instructive works, private study was the inevitable result—private study conducted in secret places, with bolted door, bated breath, palpitating heart, and wide open, alert ears. These studies resulted in a sonnet to " The North Star," printed all in capitals (I could not write) in an old Letts' Diary, and a play—a real play—called "Rosamund." I am afraid it was an awful crib. I was author, stage-manager, and cast combined. As the King, I, with a reel of silk, and the bedroom chairs, constructed a maze, winding in and out, and round about, and in its innermost recesses I hid my darling, my Rosamund. Then, as the revengeful Queen Eleanor, I discovered the clue, followed it to the centre, and stabbed my rival in the heart and the big arm-chair, or made her drain the poisoned bowl. I varied the entertainment, sometimes despatching the wicked one with the poison, sometimes with the dagger, sometimes, with an over elaboration not to be entirely commended, with both. Having a pretty and practical idea of theatrical effect, I conducted a very successful and strictly private season in an old cane chair, where, with a sheet of paper over the back, and a piece of rushlight (purloined, I am afraid) on the seat, I produced a thrilling drama entitled, "The bridge is broke and I can't get over." I do not claim originality for this production (I recollect distinctly seeing it in a "gallanty" show in Goswell Road), I simply availed myself of its suggestions. Greater than I have done this thing before, and since. I cut my scenery and *dramatis personæ* from paper. There was a bridge of abnormal elevation in the centre—Early Norman—over which was travelling an old man with a horse and cart, and under it swam a lot of ducks. I fancy the bridge broke, and the old man fell through. But I certainly recollect having considerable trouble in arranging the dialogue—unparliamentary language from the old man, quacks of alarm from the ducks, and neighs of dissatisfaction from the horse, being some of the effects which I found a difficulty in carrying out simultaneously. I had better say "right here" that my mother, discovering the MS. of the "North Star" and "Rosamund," incontinently seized and destroyed them, rewarding the daring author with smart slaps on the bare back and arms, low bodices and short sleeves (the mode in those days) making this process exceedingly practicable. I cannot understand myself—perhaps Mr. Ibsen could explain—from whence I derived my theatrical proclivities. Not from my immediate progenitrix, who thought the theatre the ante-room to hell (of course, I did not know that then, but I do now). When about eight years old, I was discovered with the unlawfully requisitioned rushlight behind me, dancing to my own shadow on the wall. My mother and a favourite uncle of mine, just up from the country, stood unobserved watching the performance with horror. Suddenly my practice was interrupted by the voice of my uncle: "Good God, Priscilla, you have let that child go to a playhouse." Well, I never had been in a playhouse, and when in after years I played my first part, Azucena, in "Il Trovatore," at the Theatre Royal, Drury Lane, I had not been inside half a dozen theatres in my life.

Did I say I was born in Islington? No? Well, I was, and though not exactly the "Bailiff's Daughter of Islington," still, my father having been a lawyer, I am something like it. I must tell that I could always sing. It was a dreadful thing for me when people came to drink tea at our house. My reputation had spread, and I would be asked to favour the company. "Now, Emily, be a good girl, and do as you're bid." And so, behind my mother's black silk apron, I sat, a tiny trembler, and trilled out my little stave, and many kisses and caresses (which I hated) were my reward. The only theatre I ever went to as a child was "Sadler's Wells." These were solemn events and much discussed for months beforehand. Every day, sometimes twice or thrice a day, Mr. Phelps, going to and from his home in Canonbury Square to the theatre, would pass along Duncan Terrace. He was a familiar and revered figure to me—sad and sedate, his hands clasped behind him, his head a little bent, his black hair rather long, and turned under at the ends. I regarded him with the greatest awe, wonderment, and envy, and stood aside, and watched, and sometimes followed close at his heels, and felt I would like to touch him, or, running on in front, turned and came slowly back, so that I could look up in his face. Another gracious figure for me was Mr. Henry Hoskins. I thought him nearly as handsome as my own father, and when I saw him at "Sadler's Wells" play "Cassio," I felt—! Ah, what would I not give if he could only be one of my uncles. These were the days when the New River ran, bright and sparkling, through the Terrace, and the big trees—as you crossed the City Road—were full of birds, busy, chattering, singing sparrows, sing,

sing, singing, always singing with full, tuneful, bursting throats. Such flights of them, such a chorus. How they flew and fought, and chirped and chipped and cheeped, and preened their brown, glossy wings, and hid themselves among the thick leaves, and peeped out with bright, black, beady eyes, so pretty. Then under the shadow of the trees, at the corner, sat a delightful person, a fruit-seller, with a big basket full of big cherries, ripe, rosy, juicy cherries, and stuck all round the basket were tall sticks, on which were tied with cotton more cherries, beautiful cherries, sometimes white-hearts, sometimes black-hearts, all lovely and shining. She used to breathe on and then polish them with a soft and tender, very tender, rag. I saw her, and sometimes she would have strawberries, ripe strawberries, pottles of strawberries, " Fourpence a pottle, strawberries." But there was more paper in the pottles than strawberries. I know, I had practical experience. Ah, well! the shining river, the actor, the strawberries, the cherries, the cherry-seller, the birds, the child, are all gone, and the trees are old, leafless, and dusty, and nothing is left but a woman and her memories.

SYDNEY, NEW SOUTH WALES.

CHAPTER I.

I hear Santley—Adelina Patti's first appearance—Her portrait in Weippert's window—I am articled to Mr. Howard Glover—Anecdotes of his mother, the great Mrs. Glover—Mr. Glover's terms—His teaching—My début at a concert, St. James's Hall, 1864—My first appearance on the stage, Drury Lane, January, 1865—My nervousness—My first impression of the Canterbury Hall—Engaged as Miss Fitz-Henry to sing at the Oxford Music Hall, 1865.

WHEN quite young, I heard Santley. Never shall I forget it. I felt I would give the world to sing, to study, to be an artist. I attacked the home authorities with vigour, and demolished all objections triumphantly. How well I remember the day I was taken to Chelsea, to Mr. Alfred Mellon, to have my voice tried. It was the day after Patti's début, 1861.

I had read in the morning paper how she, an unknown singer, had appeared at Covent Garden the previous night, in "La Somnambula," to a frigid audience, which, before the opera was half through, became an enthusiastic one.

At the corner of Regent Street (Oxford Circus)

stood at that time Weippert's music shop, and, while waiting for the Chelsea 'bus, I saw in their window a picture of the new Diva. She was not pretty in those days, but her eyes were fine, large, dark, velvety and sympathetic. Her face was long and thin, her chin, too, was long—very long and underhung; she wore her hair in plain bands, a dark dress high to the throat, and a broad linen collar.

No appointment having been made with Mr. Mellon, when we arrived at Chelsea we found him "not at home," and I returned to Islington a disappointed, sad-faced girl.

Three years after I was articled for two years to Mr. Howard Glover, an accomplished musician and linguist, a cultured gentleman, musical critic of the *Morning Post*, and son of the celebrated actress, Mrs. Glover. My master was very fond and proud of his mother, and often talked about her, and what a wonderful artistic life hers had been, though, from a domestic point, it was a failure.

Mrs. Glover was a Betterton, her marriage was a not particularly fortunate one. Her husband used to draw and squander her salary, until it was arranged she should draw it herself in advance. She had rooms over Jeffery's, the music shop in Soho

Square, on the site of which now stands the Roman Catholic Church of St. Patrick. Among her most cherished belongings was a valuable oil-painting, a portrait of herself. When Mrs. Glover went starring in the provinces, Mr. Glover's favourite diversion was pawning his wife's picture, which Mrs. Glover would on her return redeem. Mrs. Glover had the privilege of supporting all her family; charming artiste, lovely woman and loving mother, these responsibilities did not disturb her to any great extent. Still, she would sometimes jump over the traces, and I heard one very funny story of maternal revolt. It seems that during her frequent absences the housekeeping was carried on by running accounts with the tradesmen, and that on one occasion, after a dreadful journey in the winter from Dublin, on looking over the bills, she, with a loud exclamation, threw them from her, and lifting her eyes and arms to heaven, broke forth with tragic violence: "Oh, my God," cried she, "that I should cross that d——d Irish Channel to pay a thieving fishmonger twenty-four shillings for winkles!"

Mrs. Glover was a very domesticated woman, and when she came home from a country engagement, the first thing she did was to pin up her skirts, call for a broom, and, as she said, "sweep out the devil's corners." During some part of her career she received pupils, among them being a Miss Nathan—now Mrs. J. B. Howard, of the Edinburgh and Glasgow Theatres—Miss Adams, and Miss Fortesque, and the great Mrs. Nesbitt would occasionally come and go through a new part with her. Mrs. Glover only admitted two classics to her classes—Walker's Dictionary and Shakespeare. Shakespeare was not Bowdlerized in those days, and whole pages of our divine William would be carefully pinned together. Of course, the pupils took the first opportunity of pulling the pins out, reading the passages, and replacing the pins in the original holes. Mrs. Howard told me, " Mrs. Glover was a patient teacher and full of good-humour." Her first step was to make the aspiring pupil read something from Shakespeare —not the usually hackneyed selections—but something not generally known. At the lessons Mrs. Glover would hear each pupil separately, correct them, and then go over it herself, giving the proper inflections and action.

Mr. Howard Glover told me how particular they were in his mother's day about the stage business, and how all the situations and positions of everyone engaged in the scene (the "star" excepted) were marked on the floor with chalk.

In those times they worked the artistes pretty well. For instance, Mrs. Glover would appear in the opening farce, sing and dance between the pieces, and finish up with a three or four or five act drama.

My terms with Mr. Glover were 200*l*. in cash and half my earnings during my articles. Strange to say, I took my first lessons in the drawing-room over Jeffery's shop in Soho Square, the same room (Mrs. Howard has since told me) in which the girls in Mrs. Glover's time had their lessons. Mr. Glover was a careful and conscientious teacher, he not only attended to the musical part of the lesson, he cultivated my intellect, making me read, and recite, and comprehend, and understand the words of each study before commencing the notes. He was very particular about sounding all the consonants, more especially the finals. I remember, with reference to those troublesome finals, saying to him: " Isn't it dreadfully difficult to say 'ham and eggs'?"

To which he replied, " Well, I should think it dreadfully difficult to say anything else."

With all his goodness, he was impatient, and when I sang a wrong note at one lesson, and was corrected sharply, at the next (though knowing it perfectly at home) I would repeat the error through sheer fright.

A great and invariable text of my master's, and from which he preached innumerable sermons, was "The foundation of all art is nature."

In 1864, I made my début at a morning concert at St. James's Hall, at which Adelina Patti, Mme. Grisi, Mme. Albani, Sims Reeves, Mme. Guerrabella (now Miss Genevieve Ward), and most of the great foreign artistes, in London for the season, appeared. Mr. Glover accompanied me; I stood in front of the piano close to his right hand, and, when I saw the audience, felt paralysed. The symphony (rather a long one) was played, but I, frozen rigid, could not force a sound from my lips. My master, leaning forward, whispered with suppressed rage, "Go on." I was afraid of him, the whisper struck me like a blow, and I went on. I sang a composition of Mr. Glover's, "The strain I heard in happier days." My voice was good, I was a natural singer with sensibility. I made a good impression and got good notices (not entirely uninspired probably). During the season I sang at several concerts (for nothing), and it was at the Crystal Palace, under the baton of M. August Manns, I earned my first five-pound note, singing "Nobil Signor," from Meyerbeer's "Huguenots," with great success.

In January, 1865, I made my first appearance on

any stage, playing at a morning concert of Mr. Glover's, given in Drury Lane Theatre, the part of Azucena in the second act of " Il Trovatore." The Manrico was the late Mr. Swift. Mr. Glover conducted. The *Daily Telegraph* was particularly good to me. Here is what it said :—

"The matinée, however, was marked by a début which deserves some special notice. It is so seldom, indeed, that we find histrionic talent in our English vocalists, that we are bound to call attention to every instance in which a young singer evinces any capacity for acting. That Miss Emily Soldene, a pupil of Mr. Howard Glover, has dramatic stage capability of a high order, was abundantly manifested in the long scene from ' Il Trovatore ' in which she, on this occasion, made her first appearance on any stage. That she possesses, too, the physical advantages of a handsome face and tall well-proportioned figure was sufficiently perceptible through the dusky disguise of Azucena. In voice she is almost equally well gifted, and she has evidently been carefully trained."

I must have been a very emotional person in those days.

In the first flush of delight, finding by the papers I was not a failure, but rather the other thing, I forgot my fear of him, became effusive, and sent off post haste the following note to Mr. Glover.

"CARO MAESTRO,—I lay my success at your feet. Accept the offering of
"Your grateful pupil,
"EMILY SOLDENE."

I went on for this part without any actual stage preparation. Mr. Glover was anxious about the vocal rendering, but said he would trust the acting to my dramatic instinct. One morning he took me on the stage at Drury Lane to show me how to "throw" my voice. "Now," said he, "I want you to realise that at the back of that top gallery," pointing upwards into the huge dark space, "there is a small boy anxious to hear what you will sing to him—*pianissimo*, mind—in fact, a whisper. Come, try, let him hear, a pure sound, mouth well open, words clear, distinct but *pian-is-simo*."

And that is how I learnt to get at the man in the back row, no matter how big the theatre may be. In connection with this event, for of course (to me) it was an event, I must mention the great aid and assistance I got mentally, morally, and physically, from two dear, good, kind friends, the late Miss Lavine, of the Strand Theatre, and one of the original members of Miss Marie Wilton's

Company, when she opened the Prince of Wales Theatre, Tottenham Court Road, and the late Miss Harriet Coveney. They believed so thoroughly in me, that presently I began to believe in myself. They went to the theatre with me, made me up, dressed me, lent me courage, and certain mystic amulets, which, worn upon my arms and round my neck, should bring me luck.

After this I made decided progress, singing in public frequently, but always suffering exceedingly from nervousness; a nervousness distressing on the stage, but absolutely paralysing on the platform. Mr. Glover said if I did not get into regular work I should never do justice to myself or to him. At this time the only form of musical entertainment outside the Royal Italian Opera, an intermittent season of English Opera at Covent Garden, and the big concerts at St. James's Hall, were little musical burlettas and farces at the Haymarket. Mr. Glover tried, but unsuccessfully, to place me at the Haymarket. Then he had what he considered a "happy thought." I should go to Mr. Charles Morton at the Oxford, get, if possible, an engagement, sing every night, and conquer my emotional enemy, instead of allowing it to conquer me.

At this period I had never been inside a music

hall, had very lofty ideas, great ambitions, highly strung aspirations, great dreams of future glory and achievements. Going to sing at a music hall was indeed a come-down. It hurt my "artistic pride." But I swallowed my artistic pride, and armed with a letter from Mr. Glover (written on *Morning Post* official paper), I presented myself under the *nom du théâtre* of Miss FitzHenry to Mr. Morton. That arbiter of my immediate destiny was pleased to look upon me with favour, and Mr. Jongmanns, the conductor, was instructed to hear me sing, and an appointment was made; I was to go to the Canterbury for that ordeal.

Going to the Canterbury was dreadful. I remember the shock I got when I went under the railway arch, down the dingy, dirty, narrow street, the greasy sidewalk, the muddy gutter, full of dirty babies, the commonplace-looking public-house. I felt I could not go in; but I did. The people were polite, and showed me upstairs; there was lots of sawdust. Soon I found myself in a long picture-gallery, at the other end of which a rehearsal was being held. The pictures delighted, but the smell of beer and stale tobacco smoke revolted me. I have since been told that on that day I carried my head very high, and by my manner conveyed the utmost scorn for the

Canterbury and all its surroundings. "Why, what's this, Ferdy?" asked Mr. William Morton, as I appeared in the dim distance and proceeded to sail up the gallery. "Dashed if I know," said Ferdy (Mr. Jongmanns), "sent on by der governor; but it's all right if it can sing."

I sang. Mr. Jongmanns approved my vocal capabilities. I was engaged to the Oxford to sing "a turn" of songs; also in the "selections," at a salary of—well, never mind. I made my appearance, was a success, and within a year of signing my articles, began earning a regular salary.

CHAPTER II.

My musical surroundings prior to 1866—The great artistes of the Italian Opera Houses at that time—Début of Christine Nilsson—Début of Carlotta Patti—First appearance of Miss Minnie Hauk—First appearance of Ilma di Murska—Gounod's "Ave Maria" first sung at Her Majesty's—First season of Mme. Lucca—First performance of Meyerbeer's "L'Africaine"—Naudin and Lucca—Little personalities of great artistes—Mme. Sherrington's stage curtsey.

To excuse my seeming impertinence towards my Canterbury surroundings, I must explain the musical environments that for a few months I had been accustomed to, and the sort of glamour that formed a part of my professional education.

As musical critic of the *Morning Post*, Mr. Glover had at his disposal a box at each of the opera houses—Her Majesty's, then under the management of Mr. Mapleson; conductor, Signor Arditi; and Covent Garden, manager, Mr. Gye; conductor, Michael Costa. Mr. Glover, considering it to my advantage to hear as much good music as possible, sent me to one or the other of the opera houses every night of the season. There my taste was formed and nourished by the greatest artistes of the day. Then for the first time I heard Mme. Tietjens, that grand singer to whom time has brought no successor, before whose greatness I could have fallen down to kiss the hem of her garment; Trebelli, Mongini, Guiglini, and Mario. Mario was then beginning to sing out of tune, but five minutes of perfect music, which we got now and then, was compensation for all the false intonation. Then his enunciation was clear, distinct, every syllable full and round, plain, and pure. At this moment I can see him as the Duke in "Rigoletto," making his exit over the bridge, debonair, elegant, and hear his exquisite voice dying in the distance, "La don-na-e mo-bile." The last time I heard him was in that *rôle*, and it lingers on my memory still. And Delle Sedie, *there* was a singer! When he sang "Eri Tu," big tears tumbled out of my eyes, I could not help it. Such moments are impossible to describe. They can only be remembered. When I listened to all this passion, and pain, and joy, and ecstasy, a sort of despair came over me as I realised that such heights were only for the divine few. I heard Tamberlik and Viadot Garcia in "Le Prophète"; Grisi in "Norma" and "Lucrezia Borgia"; Patti in "Il

Barbière," "La Gazza Ladra," also in "Il Trovatore," in which she was not good, as it was rather out of her line. I was present when Christine Nilsson, then a tall, slender girl, with wonderful pale eyes, made her début. It was between the acts of the opera she sang, if I mistake not, "Ophelia's Mad Scene," and Eckert's "Echo Song," to the pianoforte accompaniment of Mr. Benedict. I heard Carlotta Patti on the occasion of her first appearance in England. She also sang between the acts of the opera. Mr. Benedict accompanied her. He brought her on from the O.P. side. She did not show her lameness much, as she did not come to the centre of the stage, but stood on the left of the people, looking from the front. She sang the "Queen of Night" song from Mozart's "Magic Flute" and the "Laughing Song" from "Manon Lescaut." I assisted at the first appearance of Miss Minnie Hauk, an American prima donna. The over-refined and *blasé* habitués of Her Majesty's were not then educated up to the English-speaking singer. Miss Hauk had rather hard luck, and no success. Some years afterwards she became, and still is, a celebrity. I remember the first appearance of Mme. Ilma di Murska. It was at Her Majesty's. On the night previously to her début she occupied a little box very near the ceiling, wearing a black velvet dress, and was decidedly insignificant. She appeared in "Lucia di Lammermoor," looking painfully thin, undecided, and straw-coloured, wearing a white muslin skirt, black velvet bodice, Scotch cap with eagle's feather, and a plaid fastened on the shoulder with a big buckle; she had a huge crinoline, and as she came down the rake of the stage the crinoline wobbled, and her skirt being rather long in the front, she stepped on it and stumbled forward in the most awkward embarrassing manner. She had no reception, her opening recit was half a note sharp, making everybody shiver; but when she came to the *cadenza* she executed a *tour de force* of the most startling description—coruscations, cascades, a flight of sparkling fireworks; such daring, dashing, successful *staccato* passages had never been heard before. The whole house rose and raved their applause. Her triumph was complete, and the next night Mme. di Murska did not occupy a box on the sky line, but a large one on the grand tier, and received the congratulations of a titled and *dilettanti* crowd.

The first time Gounod's air on Bach's first prelude (Ave Maria) was publicly heard in England, I was present. It was at Her Majesty's.

Mme. Tietjens sang it, and Mme. Arditi, sister of the conductor, played the violin *obligato*.

I remember the first season of Mme. Lucca—a beautiful woman, with lovely blue eyes and black lashes. She was the first brunette Marguerite Covent Garden had ever seen. There was a great movement of surprise, and conservative people were quite shocked when she came on with unorthodox long, black braids nearly down to her heels. She was a great fact, and London, at least opera-going London, mourned dreadfully when one morning the wilful prima donna was missing. She had run away to the Continent; she couldn't stand the English fog.

About this time, too, I used to see a good deal of a well-known amateur singer. He was tall, good-looking and very Byronic about the throat, wearing a turn-down collar and a loose black tie with flowing ends. His dark hair was thrown back from his high forehead in a very *dégagé* style. I am afraid I used to admire him a little, I think I should have admired him more if he had not been a trifle knock-kneed. His name was Mr. Tom Hohler; he subsequently married her Grace the present Dowager Duchess of Newcastle.

I was at the first representation of "L'Africaine," at Covent Garden. The house was magnificent—overflowing. No boxes for the critics that night. Mr. Glover gave me his stall, and he, with Mr. J. L. Davidson, musical critic of the *Times*, went into the gallery. Mme. Arabella Goddard (Mrs. Davidson) had the next stall to me. It was a night of nights. Mme. Lucca was "Selika," and M. Naudin "Nelusco." The sensation created by the unison passage for the violins in the last act is almost incredible. Everybody stood up, the enthusiasm was marvellous; and the roar of applause was like the booming of the sea.

Then, at Her Majesty's, an immense success was made by the Sisters Marchisio, whose duet-singing has never been approached—I don't know about before, but certainly not since. Their *pièce de résistance* was "Semiramide." The "Giorno d'Orrore" was worth walking ten miles to hear—such equality of time, such perfection of tone. They breathed identically together, every two notes beautifully blended—two voices of one perfect, and exquisite concord.

All these things filled me with impossible ambitions, producing sometimes an exaltation of feeling positively painful. This was the sort of Fool's Paradise I dwelt in when I went to "have my voice tried" at the Canterbury—such sublime imaginings, such sordid realities. Still, I was not always in the clouds, and during intervals of my hero-worship could not help noticing (as girls will do) that the greatest of people are not without their little personal peculiarities. For instance, there was Mme. Artot, a chic, piquant, pretty little French lady, and perfectly adorable as the Page in the "Ballo in Maschera." She was very conscious and very proud of what to my unsophisticated, ignorant eyes, was a dreadfully disagreeable and undesirable decoration—the longest finger-nails I had ever seen then, or have ever seen since, except on the fingers of a Chinese bank-teller in the Shanghai Bank, San Francisco, or an American millionairess of the first generation.

Then I could not help seeing, and hating myself for doing so, that Mme. Tietjens' corsets were dreadfully stiff, laced dreadfully tight, and audibly creaked; that she never appeared without a lace pocket-handkerchief, princess or peasant, it was all the same; that alike in the agonies of Donna Anna, in the grandeur of Fidelio, in the dungeon of Marguerite, clinging to the Cross in "Robert le Diable," or frantically entreating her lover in the "Huguenots," she carried her costly *mouchoir*, and her coiffure under any stress of emotion or danger, was always perfect, not a hair disturbed. On the other hand, Mme. Grisi, so inimitable and careful in her art, was careless to a fault as to her personal appearance, and never, even at a morning concert, had her bonnet quite straight. I was much attracted by Mme. Sherrington, a charming artiste, but artificial and perfect to faddishness in deportment. From her, by close observation, I acquired the effective stage curtsey. When you find your audience flabby and not inclined to rise to the occasion, this is how you manage them. You finish your *aria*, you bow slightly. They, rather bored, applaud slightly, you bow somewhat deprecatingly right and left, then a little lower full front. They applaud more, you repeat the manœuvre, but show no signs of going off. They applaud rather vigorously, you convey by gesture how utterly unworthy you are of so much distinction. , They appreciate such delicacy of feeling, and applaud vociferously, loudly, continuously, rapturously. Now is your time to retire, you bow and bow, and, always keeping your face to the audience, slowly exit, kissing your hands and overcome. Thunders of applause and acclamations—" Brava," " Brava," " Bravissima," " Bis," " Bis." Of course you take your call and your encore, you have earned it.

CHAPTER III.

My first hits at the Oxford, "Up the Alma's Heights" and "Launch the Lifeboat"—Mr. Charles Morton, his early career—The old Canterbury of 1848 and 1850—The new Canterbury of 1854—The picture gallery—Haydon the painter—His disappointment—His death—The Canterbury Company in 1854—Operatic selections—Visit of Mme. Tietjens—Who Cora Pearl was—Engagement of Sam Cowell—Sam Collins and Mackney—The Oxford Organisation—Artistes engaged there, 1866-1867.—Burning of Her Majesty's Theatre, December, 1867.

I WENT to the Oxford in the autumn of 1865, and "Up the Alma's Heights," a declamatory song, written by Capt. G. W. Colomb, was my first real hit. All the military men in London came to hear it. "Launch the Lifeboat," by Alfred Plumpton, was the second. All the naval men in London came to hear that. I soon got used to the people, the place, the management, and the manager. Mr. Charles Morton, as he has subsequently told me, is a self-made man risen from the ranks, and his career has been and is an active and interesting one. In 1840 he was employed at the St. George

Tavern, Belgrave Road, a sporting house, where sweepstakes of three or four hundred pounds were often made up. Among the constant visitors and most interested in the drawings, were Mr. George Hogarth, the eminent critic, and Mr. Pierce Egan, the author of "Tom and Jerry." It was the house of call for the Royal servants from Buckingham Palace, who frequently had "a bit on." "I often dined at the Palace," said Mr. Morton. Seeing me speechless with astonishment, he kindly explained, " With the cooks, I mean. And many a time after a great extra spread have I very early in the morning passed the door of Her Majesty's private apartments, laden with a table-cloth full of delicacies from the Royal table to take home to the wife and family." In 1848, he took the Canterbury Tavern, where, in the rear, was held every Saturday a "free and easy." Mr. Morton introduced an innovation—he engaged a professional singer. The business grew too big for its place, so he built a hall on the ground level, the first stone of which was laid in 1850 by two children—Lily, daughter of Mr. Morton, and Marie Grey, daughter of the landlord. The business still grew, and in 1854, out of the pothouse of 1848, he raised a temple to music and the arts by building over the first hall a second, and adding to it a picture gallery, which, being quickly filled with statuary and oil-paintings, made a great sensation, and was christened by George Augustus Sala, and known ever after as "The Royal Academy over the water."

The first lot of pictures were lent by Mr. Gambart, then of Berners Street, Mr. Morton subsequently purchasing the greater part of them. The most important work in the gallery was Haydon's "Martius Curtius," which now hangs in Gatti's Restaurant, Villiers Street, down by the side of Charing Cross Station. Mr. Morton knew Haydon intimately, and told me the painter considered the "Martius" his masterpiece. When the picture was first painted, the position of the horse was much criticised, and occasioned so much controversy that Haydon took a room at the Egyptian Hall, and exhibited his work publicly. For a time all went well, artists, critics, and the public flocked to see the much-discussed "Gee-gee." But there came along an American man, Mr. Phineas T. Barnum, who, renting the next room to "Martius Curtius," introduced to an admiring British public General Tom Thumb. Thousands rushed to see the midget, nobody ever thought of "Martius," the noblest Roman of them all drew no more shillings, and the poor painter, disappointed and disgusted, shot himself.

Soon after the completion of the big Canterbury Hall, came the operatic selections. The first one given was from " Il Trovatore," with Miss Russell, Mr. Augustus Braham, and Signor Tivoli. At the Canterbury Gounod's " Faust " was first heard in England, and so uncertain were people as to its merits, that Mr. Mapleson and Mme. Tietjens went there to hear it previously to its production at Her Majesty's. Among the singers engaged was Mr. Alberto Lawrence, an excellent baritone, who afterwards joined the Pyne and Harrison Company, and sang the *title rôle* in " Helvellyn," produced at Covent Garden Theatre. Mr. Lawrence is now a much appreciated vocal professor in New York. There too Mrs. Johnson (who in 1871 was chorus mistress at the Philharmonic) sang ballads with conspicuous ability and success. To the new hall, from the " Grecian Saloon," where, associated with Robson and Wilson (a well-known Scotch tenor), he was singing the comedy parts in English opera, came Sam Cowell. This was his first music hall engagement, and " Vilikins and his Dinah," and " The Ratcatcher's Daughter " made themselves an abiding home, and became the classics of the New Cut. Mackney and Sam Collins were also engaged, and the place became the talk of London. But these artistic successes of Mr. Morton's management did not deter him from seeing that the hungry supperer's chop was done to a turn. And with his own hands (protected by a dainty serviette) he would break the succulent baked potato on to the customer's plate, where it fell in a snowy shower, sweet-smelling, soft, floury, and hot, ye gods, so hot!

Many people whose names have since become famous strutted their little hour on the Canterbury stage. In the sixties, Miss Louie Crouch, daughter of the composer of "Kathleen Mavourneen" (who died in Baltimore, U.S.A., August, 1896, aged ninety-eight), sang there. Miss Crouch was a pretty girl, and, going to Paris on a visit, never came back, but became one of the most celebrated *demi-mondaines* of the Second Empire, the notorious Cora Pearl. That was in the sixteen-button boot days, and though Cora's name was Pearl all her buttons were diamonds.

Miss Turpin, who married Mr. James Wallack, of Wallack's Theatre, New York, was a favourite soprano at the Canterbury, and among the company engaged at the old original was a little lady, a ballad singer, named Miss Kate Somers. Miss Kate Somers is now the second Mrs. Charles Morton.

When, in 1865, I went to the Oxford, selections were given every evening from the works of Verdi, Flotow, Adam, Bellini, Bishop, Donnizetti, and others. There were glees, catches, and concerted numbers from the old English masters. Locke's music to "Macbeth" was a standing dish, and put on at any and all times, when somebody was ill or got in a passion, and couldn't or wouldn't appear, for any or no reason. For even at the Oxford little contretemps would occur, and the tantrums associated with the greatest of *prime donne* were reproduced by smaller folk, with much success. In the "Macbeth" music, a little lady named Miss Kitty Tyrell distinguished herself greatly; she had a lovely high soprano voice and excellent execution. With 1867 came Offenbach's "Orphée aux Enfers," "66," and lots of other jingling ear-catching melodies.

The conductor and prima donna for both the Oxford and the Canterbury were Mr. Jongmanns and Miss Russell, the latter an artiste of exceptional ability, possessing a splendid voice, soprana drammatica, and singing with the ease, cultivation and effect of the real Italian school.

Miss Russell is a niece of the celebrated Henry Russell, the composer. She told me she was in the room when "Cheer, boys, Cheer," was written, and sent off to Shead's, the publisher, to dispose of, "And bring back the money," was an imperative condition. Taken altogether the musical organisation of the Oxford was a very complete one. Mr. St. Aubyn, formerly of the Pyne and Harrison Company, was the tenor; Mr. Green, the bass; Miss Walmisley the contralto, and Miss FitzHenry the mezzo. Alfred Plumpton (now the conductor at the Palace Varieties) and Johnny Caulfield, junior, were the pianists; Tom Melling presided at the harmonium—(poor fellow, he was drowned at York) —Tom Melling, senior, beat the drums, and was also librarian. Mr. Goff played the double bass; principal flute was Drew Dean, and principal cornet M. Paque; Mme. Charlotte Tasca, R.A.M., assisted vocally, and was solo pianiste. The chorus was small, but good, and among its members were Mrs. Bartleman, widow of the celebrated Tom Bartleman; Mr. Husk, who had been associated with some of the greatest artistes of his day, and Mr. Nolan, now the respected proprietor of a Musical and Dramatic Institute. Mr. John Caulfield, senior, formerly of the Haymarket Theatre, was the chairman. We had a ballet, the premières of which were the Misses Gunniss. I can always remember Tessie, with the wonderful hair. It was not golden, but it was "hanging down her back." "In the front row" were two beautiful girls, Miss Alice Dunning, afterwards celebrated (particularly in the States) as Miss Alice Dunning Lingard (Mrs. Horace Lingard); and Miss Wilson, subsequently known to fame as "Lardy" Wilson. At the Oxford the original "Hanlon Brothers" made their first appearance in England, producing an immense sensation in the double somersault from the shoulders of one on to the other, a feat never previously seen in this country.

Here "Jolly Nash" made his début, got stage fright and came off, but pulling himself together, went on again and won. At the Oxford "The Kiralfys," Imrie, Bolossy, and Aniola, made their first bow to an English public, creating a furore in their Hungarian dances. Previously to their "turn" Aniola would hold on to a door-post, and Imrie and Bolossy would take it in turns to work her legs up and down like a pump handle. All this was new to me, and I thought it very wonderful. Mme. Louise produced a juvenile ballet, and in it danced a wee thing, who became the celebrated "high kicker," Mdlle. Sara. Nellie Power, a pretty young girl, who had a nice mother, did a very fetching jockey song and dance. Miss Kate Santley—ah! so slender and so slim—bewitched all beholders in "The bell goes a-ringin' for Sarah." There were the "D'Aubans and Wardes;" Mr. and Mrs. Riley (Marie Barnum), "The Dancing Quakers;" Arthur Lloyd, then in his prime; John and Katie King, children of Tom King, the tragedian—Katie, such a pretty, dark-eyed, demure little Katie, afterwards became Mrs. Arthur Lloyd; Harry Rickards, Harry Randall, Edward Marshall, of "Enchanted Hash" fame; Eugene and Unsworth, "Am I right, or any other man?" Stead, "The perfect Cure;" Fred French, the great Vance, "Champagne Charlie is my name;" George Leybourne, "Up in a balloon, boys;" Louie Sherrington, Tom Maclagan, Mr. and Mrs. Brian, "The mad Butcher," and others. The first Christmas I was at the Oxford, Herr Meyer Lutz wrote especially for Mr. Morton a "Christmas Cantata." It was a great success. I had a lovely song and made an effect. The production of "Orphée aux Enfers" was a landmark, Mr. Green and myself getting great kudos out of the "Laughing" couplets. The operatic selections sung at the Oxford were carried off bodily to the Canterbury in broughams, where, when we arrived, being "called over the coals" was not an expression, but a fact; for over the coals, through a long ill-lighted underground cellar (the original old Hall of 1850) we had to go. Though not engaged for both places, when asked "to oblige," I did.

One night, in December, 1867, the carriages were stopped at the Trafalgar Square end of Parliament Street, and we saw a magnificent sight—the burning of Her Majesty's Opera House. To me it was dreadful, I had been there so much.

CHAPTER IV.

My experience as a singer with two names—At Exeter Hall—
Kindness of Mr. Santley—Herr Molique—Herr Reichardt
—Mr. and Mrs. Weiss—" The Village Blacksmith "—
My impressions of Mr. Jules Benedict—When he accompanies me—A disagreeable conundrum—Answered by a
disagreeable pupil.

I MUST mention that while engaged in overcoming my nervousness at the music hall, I did not neglect my more aristocratic chances, and in the afternoon Miss Emily Soldene would appear at St. James's Hall, Hanover Square, or Willis's Rooms, and in the evening Miss Fitz-Henry would clamber " Up the Alma's Heights " to a top A at the Oxford. Also I was not without my Exeter Hall experiences, for being personally approved of by Sir Michael Costa, I sang in " Elijah " and the " Messiah " in company with Mr. Sims Reeves and Mr. Santley (I forget the prima donna's name). My nervousness still pursued me, and when Mr. Santley took me up on the platform, I felt a sort of comfort in confiding to him my miserable and trembling state. "Nervous," said he, "What for? You see that crowd of people in front; well, little as you know, they know less."

In these days I had a great friend in Herr Molique, such a dear old man, wearing such an impossible wig, which he had outgrown. It was rusty brown, and half up the back of his head between the edge of his wig and the tall collar of his old-fashioned coat was a vast red, wrinkled, crinkly, and uncovered expanse. But all that did not stop me liking and admiring him.

Another celebrity I used to see very often was Herr Reichardt, the composer of "Thou art so near and yet so far," a song he had written ages before, but from which he was still drawing a royalty of 400*l.* a year—at least, so people said. He was a nice, handsome, well-preserved man, with a frock coat buttoned up like a diplomat, and a soft, melancholy manner. This season I heard Mr. Weiss electrify people by singing his own song, "The Village Blacksmith," with such an immense bass voice, and such a splendid delivery. I heard him sing many times after, but cannot seem to recollect anything but "The Village Blacksmith." Mme. Weiss was a tall, thin lady, with a very perfect coiffure and an immaculately cold manner. She sang very high-toned German Lieder, in a very high-toned voice. Somehow she did not get so close to one's heart as the Blacksmith, particularly when he fancied he could hear his dead wife's voice in the village choir.

Mr. Jules Benedict, to oblige my master, would sometimes consent to accompany me at these fashionable and blood-curdling entertainments called "morning concerts." To be accompanied by that all-potent person gave a *cachet*, a sort of diploma of merit, to a young singer. He used to take me up on the platform with an ill grace, his head bent down, his under lip protruding. I was dreadfully frightened of him, and at such moments felt I would like to sink through the floor. He was very impatient, always in a hurry; and when your hands shook and you mixed up the copies, he would say, "Um," "Um," in such a tone that the chances were you dropped the lot. He was a great artist and musician, but liked to make money, I think. He had heaps of pupils. One day somebody said, "Can any one tell me when Benedict goes to sleep?" "Why, of course, didn't you know?" replied one of the disagreeables. "When he's giving a professional rate lesson, to be sure."

CHAPTER V.

The Oxford Music Hall, 1866-1867—The Chappies and the Johnnies—The table of the chairman—The racing men—My tip for the Derby, 1867—How and why the Marquis of Hastings was ruined—Pony Moore and Mrs. Moore, of the Moore and Burgess Minstrels—His benefit—Her diamonds—His ball—" Happy be thy dreams "—Mr. Howard Glover—Visits the Oxford—Miss Russell's anxiety as to what he thinks—I sing at Glasgow—Total Abstainers' Saturday Night Concerts—The City Fathers' remarks on my dress—" Davie Brown's "—A visit to Loch Lomond—A Scotch mist—" Braxey " mutton—Mr. John Ryder at the Queen's Theatre—His tears—The Oxford burnt, February, 1868.

THE Oxford was a cosmopolitan place, and the audience also was cosmopolitan, and various in its tastes and tendencies.

The Hall, a magnificent structure in the Italian style, was beautifully decorated with frescoes, gilding, and lots of light. Bars down the side were dressed with plenty of flowers, coloured glass, and any amount of bright, glittering, brass-bound barrels, and bottles. But, after all, the brightest, most glittering, and most attractive thing about the bars (of course, not counting the drinks) were the barmaids.

Rows of little tables, at which people sat and smoked, and drank, filled the auditorium, and in and out the tables circulated the peripatetic, faded, suggesting, inquiring, deferential waiter, and the brisk, alert, "cigar," "programme," and "book of the words" boy. The cigar boy of my time is now the respected manager of the Holborn Restaurant, Mr. "Tommy" Hamp.

Of course there was a certain amount of "gay" society, the "Chappies" and "Johnnies" of that period. And the "Daughters of Joy" were not conspicuous by their absence. No doubt most good people think that excess of fortune and lots of drink may induce ossification of the heart and memory in these poor girls. They are wrong, and many a night have I, "by request," sung "Home, Sweet Home," because "I made 'em cry." I daresay these were "off nights," but there is the fact for what it is worth.

The table of the chairman was a sacred place—sacred to a certain and profitable clique, and to win the applause of these quidnuncs was the direct aim of every one appearing on the stage. Winning it, one felt one's position assured. Then with the clique went the hammer of the chairman, a most stimulating and directing factor in giving " a lead " to public opinion and applause.

The Oxford was a great rendezvous for racing men. Every night there would congregate such horsey lights as Charlie Head, Charlie Bush, John Ambrose, Billy Foster, Tom King, Jimmy Maynard, Harry Beard, Tom Cook, Ted Baylis, Teddy Brayley, Chippy Norton, Sam Belasco, Johnny Gideon, Dick Dunn, and many others. On the eve of, or after a big race, the busy hum of the betting men was nearly as loud as the voices of the singers. Down would come the hammer of the chairman, " Order, gentlemen, order." To do the gentlemen justice, they did order, and much business was the result. So you see, music was not the only thing heard at the Oxford. Sometimes one got the " correct tip," and "pulled it off." But it was not always so.

In 1866, I was a good bit to nothing on Lord Lyon, and the next month relieved the monotony by coming " a cropper " over a fancy of my own. One morning in the early part of 1867, leaving the Hall after a rehearsal, the glass doors of the Oxford Street entrance were opened from the outside by a very polite and exceptionally big man. " Thank you," said I. " What are you backing for the Derby ?' said he. " Nothing," said I. " Put your money on Hermit," said he. I told Mr. Morton, I told everybody. Mr. Morton and everybody —particularly everybody—thought it the funniest thing they had ever heard. "Hermit," "broken down," "hundred to one," "absurd." When anyone wanted to chaff me terribly, they would say: "Well, how's Hermit getting on?" This was weeks before the race. The thing must have worried me, for, more than once, in my dreams I went a-racing (I had never been to a race, only heard people talk of them), and more than once came the sound of shouting voices, "Hermit wins! Hermit wins!" As all the world knows, Hermit did win (in a snow-storm), hands down, J. Daley up. I afterwards heard that the big man who gave me the "tip" was Mr. "Bobby" Phillips, the owner's "reputed" commissioner—but of course there is always a certain amount of personal mystery attaching to the operators in those delicate and deluding manipulations incidental to a racing life.

With the tidings of Hermit's win came the information that "The Marquis of Hastings was ruined." Soon I heard hints of a tragedy. Somebody said, "Chaplin swore he'd 'break' Hastings, and now he has done it!" "Break him," said I—"why?" "Why? Because the marquis ran away with his sweetheart, Lady Florence Paget. One day she went shopping with Mr. Chaplin to Swan and Edgar's. He stopped in the trap outside the Regent Street entrance, where she went in, but didn't come out. The Marquis of Hastings was waiting for her at the Piccadilly entrance, and off they went."

Goodness knows whether it was true, but it's what people said!

These were the halcyon days of Pony Moore, "Moore and Burgess Minstrels," St. James's Hall. Once a year Pony had a benefit. *Two* performances, at which *everybody* appeared, and among the "everybodies" were Miss Russell and Miss FitzHenry. At night, after the show, Mrs. Pony Moore, wearing diamonds worth a king's ransom, would "receive." Then came a ball and a supper. Such a supper! and such a company, all the prettiest women in London, and all the best men. Dukes, earls, marquises, and lords intrigued for invites. About 4.30 a.m., Pony, mounting the table, would make a speech welcoming his guests, and finish up by telling them he was a freeborn American, and what he had paid for the champagne.

One night he handed me on to the table and begged as a great favour that I would sing a song,

"Happy be thy Dreams." I said I would. Then he sent for all his minstrels to come and take a lesson in ballad singing. When I'd finished, Pony addressed the crowd. "Great God," said he, "if that gal 'ud only sing that song in New York, in Wood's 'Muse-um,' she'd knock 'em. Great Cæsar's ghost, she'd knock 'em!" This was not very refined, but, all the same, Pony Moore's ball was one of the features of the London season, and everybody, who "by hook or by crook" could, went.

Mr. Glover, naturally anxious about my progress, would sometimes have a box and sit out the "selection." He brought back all my nervousness, and I used to be dreadfully glad when he went out. The first time he came Miss Russell was very anxious about his opinion, and the next night asked me, not "What did he think of my singing?" but "What did he think of my bust?"

During my engagement at the Oxford I, by permission of Mr. Morton, sang at Canterbury for the "Canterbury Catch Club," and went to Glasgow to the "Total Abstainers' Saturday Night Concerts." Signor Foli was singing at the same series. It was the first time I had met him, but we soon became good friends. When I told him I was married, he looked at me with the greatest astonishment, and said, "What a pity." He did not explain whether it was a pity for my husband or for myself. At that time everybody wore huge crinolines. I never allowed one near me, at least not nearer than my neighbour's skirts. The "City Fathers" had seats on the platform at the City Hall, and regarded me with much attention when I made my appearance, dressed in white satin and no petticoats to speak of. After the concert I got a message. The committee approved of "ma seenging," but thought I "deesplayed ma feegure ower much." Mr. and Mrs. Morton were in Glasgow at the same time, and we all went to "Davie Brown's" music hall. The smoke was so dense one could not see the stage at all 'til the clouds rolled by a bit. But "Davie Brown" gave us stewed rabbit for supper and a huge welcome. During the week we went to Balloch, up the loch. *Of course* there was a Scotch mist. I had a plank to stand upon, the deck of the boat being a baby river. Arrived at the head of the loch we struggled up a hillside, over the heather, the *moist* heather. The water ran down our necks and squelched out of the top of our boots with little sharp squeaks of remonstrance. Presently we came to a shepherd's hut, where the walls were like a ship's cabin lined with beds. The "bit place" was full of smoke, delicious peat or burnt wood smoke, and the wash-basin full of lovely cream-laden milk. I drank some, and it was so refreshing. My companion was horrified. "A wash-basin? Oh! she really, really could not." While there we learnt what "braxey" mutton meant. When a sheep dies on the hillside, the person finding it takes it by the head and swings it round and round. If the body does not fly off into space it is all right. If it does, why it's "braxey." When the merry Highlander wants to be hideously funny at the expense of the Saxon, he says, "Braxey's good enough for the Southerner." We got fearfully wet that day, but returning to the hotel had "whusky" inside and out, and no harm done.

So many people at this time thought me dreadfully dramatic, and said I ought to study and go on the stage, and one day, it was February 10th, 1868, I, by appointment, met Mr. John Ryder on the stage of the Queen's Theatre, to hear his opinion. He asked me, "What could I do?" I said, "Nothing." He gave me the Portia speech, "The quality of mercy, &c.," to read. After I got through, he walked up and down for a minute or two, then stopped: "You have tears in your voice," he said; "are your tears near the surface? can you cry easily?" I could not tell him.

"Look at me," said he, smiling, and, reciting a few lines, the tears ran down his face as freely and as miserably as possible. Of course I was astonished. "Come to-morrow, same time," said he; "we will have a serious lesson." But to-morrow never came. That evening I sang the last "turn" on the programme, and in the middle of the night the Oxford was burned. *I* sang the last song sung in it, and that song was, "Launch the Lifeboat."

CHAPTER VI.

At the Alhambra—Mr. Frederick Strange, manager—Mr. John Hollingshead, general manager—Mr. Rivière, conductor—Mme. Pitteri, the première danseuse, and her appurtenances—Annie Adams—Her "Indian Drum"—Her dresses—Her husband—The Vokes family—The canteen—The habitués—Mabel Grey—Pen picture of a person—I have an offer to play the "Grand Duchess"—Kindness of Mme. Pitteri—Her sad end.

AFTER the Oxford fire, I was engaged at the Alhambra, which was then a music hall, with grand ballet, and varieties. These were the palmy days of Frederick Strange. Mr. John Hollingshead was the general manager, M. Rivière the conductor, and Mme. Pitteri, a magnificent creature and great artiste, was the première danseuse. Her hair, naturally dark, was dyed a beautiful gold, quite an up-to-date proceeding then. She had a deliciously white, soft, satiny-looking skin. She told me she bathed in warm milk every day. Her dressing-room was gorgeous, decorated with *bric-a-brac* and silken hangings. She had a French maid, and an Englishwoman to wait on the maid, also a toilette service of solid silver, and magnificent presents from many persons, some of them princes. Among the variety people playing then was Annie Adams, a loud-voiced and commanding serio-comic, who sang with much vigour and more applause:

> "He played on the Indian drum-drum-drum,
> All down the street he would come-come-come,
> He played on the Indian drum-drum-drum,
> And made a most terrible noise."

She was a very big woman, with a fine figure, a pretty face, and always splendidly dressed. Her husband, Mr. Harry Wall, of copyright fame, used to wait in the first entrance with his mouth full of pins, and when she came off pinned up her skirts to keep them out of the dust. The "Vokes Family" were also of the company. They played "The Belles of the Kitchen." The family were all together then, Barbara, Victoria, Fred, Fawdon, and pretty, moonfaced, piquant, kittenish, mischievous Rosina. These were the days of "The Canteen," and the business was enormous. Among the regular habitués of the theatre was a beautiful creature, who, accompanied by her maid and half concealed by the hangings of her box, sat every night and received her courtiers; she was tall, slender, fragile, elegant, refined, and wore outrageously costly, but perfect toilettes, and some of the best diamonds in London. It was the celebrated Mabel Grey, the most notorious, extravagant, vampirish *demi-mondaine* of the day, and the original of "Skittles."

We used to have some—not many—visitors behind the scenes, and nearly every night, about 9.30, came a tall, gaunt old gentleman; his long hair was sleek and iron grey, his beard rather short, and pointed (François première), and his shoulders a little bent. He wore his hat at the back of his head, and two noticeable features of his attire were his long coat and his rich, broad, black satin neck scarf, so broad as to nearly conceal the shirt front. In this scarf glittered a priceless gem, sometimes a ruby, sometimes a pearl, sometimes an emerald set round with diamonds. On his fingers were one or two other gems, also priceless; in them he always carried a huge cigar, which he sometimes smoked (the smoking was *not* allowed behind the scenes). He talked (with a nasal accent) to the ballet a good deal, but it was understood always for their good. Indeed, he was looked upon as a regular father to the ballet, but perhaps an irregular one would be nearer the mark. If the girls admired (which they generally did) the emerald, ruby, or pearl, he told them gently it should be theirs, but for one thing : It was "a gift from a dead friend ; he could never part with it." I will not record the subsequent and disrespectful remarks of the ladies. He was quite the equal of Mr. Gilbert's Englishman in asserting his superiority to temptation of every kind, and was never weary of proclaiming his infallibility in the way of personal virtue (notwithstanding all and many inducements to the contrary), and his faithfulness to his domestic obligations. In spite of which, when unprotected female folk (especially if they were plump), came in a cab to do a "turn," he would, when they were through, offer them the accommodation of his brougham and his personal attendance. He had a great penchant for a night or two at Brussels, and on his return would present the ballet with pin boxes, card cases, and little nicknacks made of tortoise-shell, inlaid with silver. Also he brought back lots of kid gloves, "job" lots, I fancy, "reduction on taking a quantity." This old gentleman was a son of Israel, and if not universally beloved, was universally benevolent, for his ear and his purse were always open to the necessities (and the collaterals) of the upper class and impecunious Gentile.

One night he brought with him a tall, slender youth (also slightly bent about the shoulders), with a face of the highest Semitic type (beautiful, sending one's mind back to the days of the Nazarene), and a profusion of glorious, waving, bright, chestnut hair (he's not so good-looking now). His appearance was altogether perfect, so were his manners. The old gentleman said, "Miss FitzHenry, allow me to present to you my younger son; Miss FitzHenry, my son Alfred." The old gentleman was—Well, now, *who* was it? Don't all speak at once.

One night Mr. John Russell, of Covent Garden Theatre, called on me at the Alhambra. He had a company out on tour with Offenbach's "Grand Duchess" (originally produced at Covent Garden by Mr. Augustus Harris, with Mrs. Howard Paul as her eccentric highness). Miss Julia Mathews was Mr. Russell's prima donna, and I think pulled the prima donna string somewhat tightly. Anyway, Mr. Russell wanted a second possible Duchess, and asked me if I would join him. Of course I jumped with joy; anything to get out of the music hall into a theatre, a real theatre, with no smoke, no beer, no varieties, no—well, never mind. But I had a contract with the Alhambra, and Mr. Strange would not release me. It was like death losing such a chance. I went to Mme. Pitteri, whose word was law, and begged her to get me off, and she, like the lovely, kind, splendid, big-hearted woman she was, did it, and I was free to take my step. Years afterwards, asking an agent who had made much money out of the danseuse (and who licked the dust from her feet in the days of her prosperity) for news of her, he told me indifferently "she was dead." Dead in poverty and distress; died while filling an engagement in a low dance house among the sailors at Marseilles. She had spent all her money; the presents were gone, so were the princes.

CHAPTER VII.

I am engaged for the "Grand Duchess" by Mr. John Russell, of Covent Garden Theatre—Managers won't have me—Miss Julia Mathews—Falls ill—I am fetched to the Standard—I play Duchess—My costumes—My tenor—I play Boulotte in "Barbe Bleu," first time in English—The company—Mr. Augustus Harris, sen., as a singing master—We go on tour—My salary that is not a benefit—My benefit which is not a salary—I play "The Duchess" at the Crystal Palace—Messrs. Mansell engage me for the Lyceum Theatre.

MR. JOHN RUSSELL engaged Miss Emily Soldene to play the Grand Duchess, and I ascended into the seventh heaven—but soon came down again. The provincial managers would not have *me* at any price; they *would* have Miss Julia Mathews. Ah! what tears, what snubs, after I had begged out of the Alhambra and learnt the Opera in six days. For some weeks I had a dreadful time of despair, and began to think that after all there were worse things than music halls and regular salaries.

One morning Mr. Russell came in a great hurry and a cab to fetch me to rehearsal at the

Standard Theatre. Miss Mathews was ill, I must play that very night. When we arrived Mr. Douglass pooh-poohed me and my pretensions. "Too young," "no experience," "knew nothing about it," "would break down." The tenor refused to rehearse with me. But my temper, unbroken, was up to concert pitch, and I went through it without him. Then came the costume question. I had to wear Miss Mathews' dress; the skirts were considerably too short, so bands of velvet were sewn on. In the middle of the lap of the pale-blue satin military dress was a huge and highly descriptive grease spot. "Lor," says the dresser, "that hain't nothin', onny w'ere Miss Mathews puts 'er fried fish at night; she 'ave hit hafter hevery hact; nobody 'ull see hit from th' front." In the delicate "business" of the second act, Fritz, lying back in my lap, made many piano and extraneous observations calculated to break me up with either rage or tears. But he might as well have tried to disturb Lord Nelson on the top of his Trafalgar Square column. I made a success, converted Mr. Douglass, and delighted Mr. Russell. I know I sang and acted remarkably well, considering the circumstances, and after four days the tenor (I was not his "Sweetheart when a boy"—but no matter), knelt on the stage, kissed my hand, and begged the Grand Duchess to forgive him. I am glad to say her highness, taking a lenient view of the case, pardoned him on the spot; but Miss Emily Soldene has consistently disliked him ever since.

Mr. Russell was under contract to Mr. Douglass to produce in English during this engagement Offenbach's "Barbe Bleu." When I had sung ten nights, he gave me the part of Boulotte, which was my first original creation. This time Mr. Douglass did not "pooh-pooh" me. Mr. Desmond Ryan, the adapter, and the nicest man in the world, backed me up, took my part, and helped me with it. The opera and all of us were a great success. Mr. Wilford Morgan played Barbe Bleu; Mr. Aynesly Cook, Popolani; Mr. "Jimmy" Stoyle, the King; Mrs. Aynesly Cook, Queen Clementina (she was so funny, and when the king was naughty, carried him off, kicking in her arms like a baby); Mdlle. Albertazzi was the Princess, and myself Boulotte. In the cast were also: Mr. W. H. Payne, his sons Fred and Harry, and Mr. and Mrs. Oliver-Somers. The dresses were lovely, made by Mr. Augustus Harris, who, by-the-bye, had given me the most wonderful singing lesson in the "Dites lui." On the fateful morning of my first appearance at the

Standard in the evening, while I was rehearsing with the band the second act of the Duchess, Mr. Harris came on the stage, and standing in front of me, with his back to the orchestra, his hat tipped well over his eyes, his legs far apart, and both his hands in his trousers pockets, extending to their full extent his up-to-date "peg tops," said, irritably: "*Don't* sing it like that. It is not 'Say to him,' but 'Sa—y to him,'" and he sang the passage with a portando della voce, a caressing and insinuating inflection, a sigh, a pause, a catching of the breath, an intention, and (pulling his hands out of his pockets) a grace of action, that I, finding irresistible, caught on to, assimilated, and reproduced with the greatest success. It does not sound much, but it made no end of difference to the song. After the season at the Standard we went on tour. We were reinforced by Mme. Fanny Huddart (Mrs. John Russell), to play in "Nine Points of the Law," and Miss Lizzie Russell, to appear in the "Little Treasure."

We visited lots of places which I forget, but remember Bath, for there I had my portrait taken, also my watch. Then we went to Bristol, Cheltenham, and I got lots of experience, much glory, but little money. Not that the business was bad, but the treasurer was elusive, and if you wanted a little cash you had to run half over the town to always find "he'd just stepped out." And Mrs. Russell was the nicest woman, always "so sorry," and "it was too bad of John," and "I'd ask you to come in, dear, and wait, but I'm just going to bed."

It seems in those days it was the exception for people in travelling companies (and indeed in some that did not travel), to get their salaries. They got a little on account, and managers looked much astonished when it was darkly suggested by an inexperienced one that they should " settle up." Certainly, financially, things were much better arranged in music halls. I had a "benefit" at Cheltenham. The Assembly Rooms were crammed, and all the chairs for a mile round pressed into the service, but I did not touch a red cent. Still money did not trouble us (my sister travelled with me), so long as the board bill was paid. It was perfectly lovely for us two to be alone on tour; independent, with nobody to contradict or control us. In Bristol we had large rooms, such large ones, in a grey stone house, in a dismal grey stone square, near the theatre. How we did enjoy ourselves. Came home from the performance at such hours, 10.30 at least; had hot coffee and toast, and raw tomatoes, and onions sliced in vinegar; sat up reading novels as late as we liked, stopped in bed, reading novels as late as we liked; read novels at breakfast, dinner, tea and supper, a proceeding which, at home, was much discouraged and attended with penalties. There is no other word for such a state of things *but* "lovely." I had another benefit at Bristol, same financial result for me, but how I did luxuriate and revel in seeing my name in large letters on the top of the play bill, a real play bill of a real play house. The dear old Royal. No matter whatever direction I went for a walk, my willing feet always led me past the bill—"Benefit of Miss Emily Soldene—The Grand Duchess."

After wandering about the provinces for some time, we appeared at the Crystal Palace. It was there Mr. Mansell saw me play Her Highness of Gerolstein, and engaged me for Marguerite, in the forthcoming production of "Little Faust" at the Lyceum, music by M. Hervé, adapted from the French by Mr. Henry Brougham Farnie.

CHAPTER VIII.

My first impressions at the Lyceum—The part the *Daily Telegraph* played in the toilettes of the ladies—Miss Love and her mother—The Misses Egerton—Mr. and Mrs. Clarkson and their little boy—Mr. Clarkson in his "Shay"—Hervé as "Chilperic"—How he fascinated the ladies, not omitting the principal cleaner—His sensitiveness—What he died of—Mr. H. B. Farnie's devotion to the chorus (feminine)—How Mr. Dion Boucicault sought to lighten H. B.'s labours—The result thereof.

FIRST impressions, I think (at least, it is so with me), are always vivid. For instance, I recollect distinctly my first visit to the Lyceum. Being a member of the company, I went to see the show —"Chilperic"—and a very fetching kind of show I found it. I got in during the second act. The ballet was on, and exceedingly nice the ballet looked, in graceful and classical and rather diaphanous draperies, but perfectly proper—the sort of thing one might take one's mother, or, in fact, one's mother-in-law, to see. They were indulging in a wavy, dreamy, mystical movement, when suddenly, "Bing-bang-boom!" on the drums and cymbals, and to everybody's astonishment four-and-twenty legs shot out on the O.P. side as far as possible, and as undressed as possible, and, before we had recovered from this severe shock, four-and-twenty other legs shot out on the P. side, just as far and quite as nude. The dresses were worse than deceptive, they were slit up to the waist. But if the ballet was fetching, what about the Pages? Such pages! such figures—long and straight in the limbs, and soft and supple and—well, simply darlings. And their costumes! It did not take you long to see them. And one realised that with obvious advantage brevity could be applied to more things than wit. They were a bunch of graded Venuses, from the adorable five-foot-ten " Lardy " Wilson, in the centre, to the piquant and pert four-foot-nothing Jennie Lee (" Jo ") in the corner. They looked very natty, for those were bustling days, and everybody's trunks had to stand out then, as everybody's sleeves do now, and the exact and particular effect could only be arrived at by utilising a newspaper. And so every girl regarded her *Daily Telegraph*, not only as a source of information, but as a necessary and not-to-be-done-without adjunct to her nightly and personal charms, and having got through her own favourite column, she made no more to do, but tucked the

"Largest Circulation" into the most conspicuous part of her costume, and "went on," rustling and rattling, and pluming and preening herself like the proud young bird of paradise she was.

There was a particularly beautiful girl there—a Miss Love. She was a great swimmer, and she had a particularly beautiful mother, who used to be behind the scenes very frequently. I don't know whether she was a swimmer, too, but if she were, judging from her elegant appearance, she kept above water all the time. This lovely lady perpetuated her loveliness, for the lovely present Mabel Love is the lovely granddaughter of this lovely grandmamma.

Then there were the beauteous Egertons—delicious—and such a lot of them. All the girls were fair and good——. Good? Why, of course—I wish you would not interrupt—I was about to say "good gracious, wore such a lot of hair." In those days, no matter how bountiful Nature had been, if you possessed any proper pride in your profession, or the slightest spark of self-respect, you had to troop round to Clarkson's and buy a bunch of curls at least a yard long. Mr. Clarkson, sen., was alive then, short-winded and puffy, rather gruff and Hogarthian in manner and appearance; but it was all and only appearance, for his voice was soft and his disposition delightful. He used to go about with a little pony dragging him in a little cart or chaise, which was so small that you feared with every jolt he would fall off, not out, for he never seemed to be quite in. And Mrs. Clarkson was such a pretty woman, a blonde with a limited embonpoint, a lovely skin, and a pretty curly-headed boy. They say good-looking babies grow up plain, but when one regards Mr. Clarkson, jun., one realizes that the saying is an old-fashioned fallacy.

What a cast it was for " Chilperic." Hervé, in the title part, such an elegant, charming artist; such gaiety, such grace, such distinction, such perfection of style, such expressive hands, they were, if possible, more expressive than his face; not much voice, but what wonders he did with it! And then his delightfully broken English, not too broken, just broken enough, and the charming way he carried off Fredegonde, and promised to love her for ever and ever in the first act, and didn't love her at all in the second, but danced the cancan, and chaffed and aggravated her till she had hysterics, and threw her shoe at him; not a nasty, awkward, raw-hide sandal as befitted the period, but a delicious Parisian pink satin confection—No. 1¼, with a Louis Quatorze heel.

No wonder the women went down in regiments before this redoubtable foreign fascinator; at least, that's what they used to say. It was even whispered that the principal cleaner, aet. 67, was not entirely unaffected by his magnetic influence. I, of course, have no personal knowledge of such things, but I recollect congratulating myself on the fact of being engaged to sing and act with this accomplished creature. No doubt he was a charming man, but with all his pretty ways he had a great idea of his own dignity, and would not allow anyone to infringe upon it.

Once, in particular, a little lady, with a pinched-in waist, a triple-expansive bust, and a manner at once insolent and aggressive, made at rehearsal an impertinent reply to some stage direction of M. Hervé's. "Come here, ma fille," said the maestro, in a gentle, beseeching tone. "Ma fille" marched up, posing like an angry pouter pigeon. "Ah!" said he, touching the bust delicately and inquiringly with the tip of his delicate finger, "One can buy that, mais, ma foi, one cannot buy this," tapping his forehead violently, "buy this; comprenez, ma fille?—understand?"[1]

There was a good deal of French spoken in the

---

[1] He was an *excessively* sensitive man, and died in '92 of an adverse newspaper criticism.

theatre, which gave a cachet and elegance to any little eccentricities of expression that might—in fact, that did—occasionally intrude themselves into the Green Room conversazione. The late Mr. Farnie was very constant in his attendance, and was generally to be found in one of the upper entrances very much engaged with the chorus— the feminine chorus. He never allowed anything in the way of a deputy or anything else, if he could possibly help it, to come between him and the chorus. He had a very keen feeling for the beautiful, and most especially affected the Burne-Jones style of beauty, but was not bigoted. Indeed, I may mention, as showing the broad and catholic view he took of these æsthetic differences, that the best-looking girls in the theatre, even if they were a little plump, were never allowed to appeal to him in vain. As a rule, their intelligence was not on a par with their physical perfections, but this did not affect the benevolence of his intentions. And he would call a rehearsal at any extraordinary hour, and if the girls were very good-looking indeed would stop with them any length, or even give them lessons privately one at a time; but there his consideration ended, it did not extend to ordering any refreshments; that's where he drew the line, except on one occasion, when a very pretty girl (who had not had a private lesson) was shivering with the cold, he sent the call-boy for some hot brandy and water. "Oh, Mr. Farnie," said she, sniffing and sniggering, "hi'm hafraid hit will git hin me 'ead." "Probably," replied H. B., "Nature abhors a vacuum." Then he rubbed his chin and looked round for all of us to laugh. And we did. Nice cads, weren't we? Of course, this sort of thing was a great tax on his time and patience, and sometimes he would be assisted in the work by the late Mr. Dion Boucicault, who came to the theatre pretty frequently, and was understood to take a good deal of paternal interest in the young ladies' progress; of course, purely from an artistic point of view. But Mr. Farnie must have had a real regard for Mr. Boucicault, and would not allow him to be worried with the woes of the chorus, for no sooner did the girls surround this charming author-actor, and most interesting man of his day, than Farnie would clap his hands together violently, and cry out, "Now, girls, to your places; you'll get your cue in a moment. And, mind! I'll fine every one that's late. Do you hear?" And they did hear, and fled.

CHAPTER IX.

I play "Chilperic"—Mrs. Maitland's views on riding *à la Amazon*—A true story of Mr. Hengler—The principal ladies in " Chilperic "—Miss Emily Muir—Miss Selina Dolaro—Marius as Landry—His voice, and what he did with it—Mr. Frank Musgrove as musical director—Mr. "Johnny" Milano as stage manager.

AFTER a long run of "Chilperic" M. Hervé got fatigued—finding the evening performance and the daily rehearsals for the production of "Little Faust" too much for him; so it was suggested that I should play Chilperic. I commenced the study at once, and went through the part with M. Hervé. Chilperic makes his first entrance on horseback, and the one thing that troubled me was having to ride on to the stage *à la Amazon*. One day, talking over the matter with Mrs. Maitland (the mother of Messrs. Mansell), she soon put me at my ease. "Me dear Soldene," said she, with the least taste in life of the brogue, "It is nothing; when I used to hunt in Ireland and came to a bit of stiff country, we women simply picked up our habits (long in those days) so

—threw our right leg over, so—and there you are. It's nothing in the world, I assure you, nothing in the world, me dear!" Mrs. Maitland was a charming lady, a fascinating woman, a bit of a Bohemian, and a tremendous smoker, not of cigarettes but cigars. Her hands and arms were exceedingly white and well formed, she wore loose sleeves falling back from the elbow, and the smoking business showed her off to great advantage.

Reassured by such counsel, I rode on the stage in such style, that the men in the front forgot I was a girl, and also forgot to laugh. Apropos of the riding, when afterwards I went to Dublin with "Chilperic," Mr. Hengler was playing there, and we sent to the circus to borrow a horse. He had a beautiful creature, pure white, and full of action. The terms were 3*l.* 3*s.* per week, and 10*s.* for the groom. "But," said he to my stage-manager, "I will come to the Gaiety to-night, and if Miss Soldene mounts the horse properly on the stage, tell her it shall cost her nothing." And it did cost me—just nothing. That horse was a darling, and learnt his cue—two trumpet calls—in two rehearsals. After the third performance, he would anticipate it and pull so desperately, that when we did get it, we went on with a rush. Chilperic has to dismount at the end of the act (during the celebrated umbrella dance), mount again and ride off. This was the crucial point alluded to by Mr. Hengler. It was rather a difficult thing to do; what with the lime-light, the lightning, the rain box, the blare of the brass, the banging of the drums, cymbals, and the whirling round and up and down of forty umbrellas, my Arab steed had all his work to do to keep quiet, and I had all my work to get on his back. But I did it. To play Chilperic at the Lyceum after Hervé was rather an undertaking, but I came out all right, and made a dashing lady-killer. The dresses suited me personally, the music suited me vocally. It was a delightful part, and I had a delightful time. The people in the theatre made no end of a fuss over my success, and the principal ladies were so kind that——But coming to the principal ladies in the original cast of " Chilperic," we have to tread with soft and tender and halting footsteps, with finger on lip and bated breath, for theirs is the dignity of silence, theirs the effacement of " Oh ! ah ! " " Oh, yes !" " Now I recollect ! " theirs the sanctification of being only a memory. They have the advantage of us later lagging ones. They have solved the great problem, have crossed the dark and sometimes troubled river, have joined the majority, have gone to that bourne—they

are dead. Will you believe me when I tell you
that, thinking of them, the quick, unbidden tears
fill up to the brim my too-well remembering eyes?
After all these years I can see them so plainly.
They stand, where? why there before me, alive
and breathing. Emily Muir was the Fredegonde,
a medium-sized girl, a cousin of Agnes Robinson,
Mrs. Dion Boucicault. Her face was decidedly
Scotch in character. It was a nice face, with
bright, merry, and inquisitive grey eyes. She had
a good deal of smart and dry humour. Once upon
a time we went to St. James's Theatre. The performance was operatic, " Maritana "—by-the-bye,
did you know that " Maritana " was an Australian
opera? Everybody, at least every Australian
body, believes in the local legend, which says that
Vincent Wallace wrote this work in a small house
or lodging in Castlereagh Street, Sydney, N.S.W.
Well, on this occasion the immoral and in-
vertebrate King of Spain was played by a son of
the late Mr. Henry Hersee. Did anyone ever
hear of anybody who ever made a success of that
particular King of Spain? I never did. Well,
anyway, young Hersee did not, and one of our
party made some up-to-date and not too flattering
remark. " Oh," said Fredegonde, " I don't think
he's so bad, see how hard he works;" and

that was the exact expression to fit the case, he did work hard. As Fredegonde, she was picturesque and rather spirituelle-looking, wearing a short white cashmere dress, with a sheepskin slung across her shoulders, and her hair (the inevitable and impossible hair), a perfect fleece, a golden-yellow-glittering glory, long and wavy, and tously, and getting into her eyes and out again in quite the most too-sweet-for-anything and fetching style. This was in the pre-Minnie-Palmer days, and Emily's "business" was original—"all her own." That fleece fell rippling down her back, in fact all round her; it was curly at the ends, and they touched the bottom of her skirts and nearly the tops of her boots, which were high red ones, laced up the front. She had nice little tootsicums, real tootsicums, one could not call them feet, they were too small. Her voice was a light soprano (soprana leggiera), and having gone through a long course at the Conservatoire, Paris, she sang in quite the French manner; and, if the truth must be told, with a good deal of tremolo. She was gay, and bright, and chippy, and charming, but on occasion could be very earnest. She had a certain amount of *finesse*, and I also certainly think she recognised the fact that two and two make four.

Then there was Dolaro, Selina Dolaro, as the

Spanish princess, with her dark Moorish face, her truly wonderful eyes, her ivory-coloured skin and red lips, carrying a flower in her mouth years before Bizet's "Carmen" was created, or even thought of. What an inimitable and Spanish and coquettish, and altogether "too too, don't you know" shake she would give to her petticoats, as she tripped down the stage. What a blaze of colour, red and yellow, and black satin, and gold spangles, and a high brass comb—such a comb was never seen before—with spangled mantilla, a red rose in her hair, and all over her little knots and fluttering bows of ribbon, and little metal tips and tabs that tinkled again, and black silk spangled stockings, and tiny shoes embroidered with gold, and a tambourine with long and sweeping ribbons — all the colours of the rainbow—and little bobs of colour at the edges of her skirts. On she would come, wearing all these things, and a mixed expression which was supposed to be at once Spanish and demure, and you believed in it, until she, lazily lifting her white heavy eyelids, you were, suddenly and certainly and completely, convinced that "demure" used in association with her was not the appropriate expression.

The Selina Dolaro of those times was not the fashionable "Dolly" that was subsequently evolved. In the days I am speaking of, she would, after the performance, make haste and get dressed (she invariably wore black), and wait on the stage in the semi-darkness for her father, Mr. Simmons, who was one of the first violins. He always came up quickly, and, catching hold of her, out they would go—out into the night—so attached, they seemed all in all to each other, the father with his daughter in one hand and his fiddle-case in the other.

There was another member of the cast who absolutely divided the palm of loveliness with the ladies. This was a masculine " masher," Marius, then young and beautiful, and slender, and sleek, and sly, and so elegant. An ideal Cherubino, but, I am afraid, even more susceptible than that operatically historical and love-stricken young person. He played Landry, and made love to Fredegonde or Brunehant, he didn't care which, with an ardour that was not only particularly French, but particularly pleasing, and particularly successful, so successful, indeed, that every girl in the front of the house was seized with a wild desire to understudy those two erratic, not to say imprudent characters. He certainly looked awfully nice, his figure being perfection. And how clever he was! and how he managed what he was pleased to call "his voice"! It was not singing, but "he got there all the same." He had a solo in the second act, and at the finish there was a top A. To see with what grace and energy he worked up to the climax, and then, at the supreme moment, rushed to the front, opened his mouth (such a pretty one, with a tiny, soft, dark line, masquerading as a moustache) as wide as possible, lifted his right arm to Heaven, looked the gallery full in the face, and sang straight from the chest—what?—nothing—not a sound; and the orchestra sustained him with a big, long, tremolando chord; and the public always encored him with acclamation, and he—he always did it again.

Frank Musgrove was the musical director; an excellent musician and charming conductor, sympathetic, and always "wid you." "Johnny" Milano was the stage manager; a good man and clever artist. In every scene and every ensemble he was on the stage, now in one costume, now in another. Under such direction it was impossible for the "business" to go wrong. Speaking from my own personal knowledge, from what up to that time I had myself seen, "Chilperic" was the most perfectly mounted and managed piece in the Opera Bouffe line that had as yet been placed upon the English stage. And speaking from my own deep sense of obligation, I must say that M. Hervé more than helped to form a style that has met with approbation for more years than it is wise or ladylike to remember; the style that rendered an English Chilperic possible, that made an English Drogan, so I have been told, irresistible.

CHAPTER X.

Mr. Tom Maclagan in Hervé's "Little Faust"—His musical eccentricities—Mdlle. Marguerite Debreux as Mephisto—Her voice—What she did with it—Professional (floral) amenities—Mr. Aynesly Cook as Valentine—Miss Lennox Grey as Wagner—How she whistled—Miss Jennie Lee as the Street Arab—The nebulous "Jo"—Mr. Charles Wilmot, "The man from New Zealand," as the Cabby—Miss Laura Morgan as the Tiger—Mr. Odell as Martha—Myself as Marguerite—Mr. Boucicault again—The girls, and how they played in school—Marius as Seibel—How he went to the Franco-German War—Mr. Hollingshead at the première—His behaviour—How I kept the stage waiting—People who came behind the scenes—Captain Harry Larkin—How he died—Where he is buried.

DID you ever dream that you fell from sunny, bright, and inaccessible heights, down—down—down for days and days and days into vast and deep and dark and unfathomable space? Well, that's the sort of fall I got when I heard that I was to play Marguerite, not to the poetical Faust of M. Hervé, but to the prosaic Faust of Mr. Maclagan, Mr. "Tom" Maclagan, who looked lovely in a kilt, and was simply perfect as a "Geordie," a "Robbie," a "Donald," or a "Sandy," but in tights, and as a substitute for Hervé, unæsthetic and awful. He had a lovely tenor voice, but was no musician, and would always "come in" in the wrong place—a bar too soon or a bar too late. One night during the performance, Mr. Musgrove, getting really angry, rapped the desk loudly with his baton, and Thomas, in a rage, rushed down to the footlights, and leaning over, shouted to the conductor, "It's a' vera weel fer you tae sit doun there awaggin' yer stick, jes' come up *here* an' du it yersel'." Imagine the roar of laughter that went up from the audience. Poor, dear Maclagan, such a good fellow, and such an out and out admirer of me, his traducer !

But if our Faust was awkward, the public were more than compensated by our Mephisto, our specially imported Mephisto, the beauteous Mdlle. Debreux. Chic and shapely, full of brand-new bouffeisms, she brought the air of the Boulevards with her, and came on tiny tripping toes, armed with diabolical devices to break up all the women and capture all the men, with a perfect figure, no corsets, and a svelte waist that waved and swayed with every movement, with manicured pink nails an inch long, with a voice that cracked and creaked like a rusty sign-board in half a gale of wind, and was never exactly there when wanted.

But these vocal eccentricities were accompanied by such grace and gesture and perfect insinuation that a little thing like C sharp for D natural was considered quite the finest art. She was an immense success, and made us English girls just "sit up," and we felt very sick indeed. I had great fun one night. In the trio of the second act, sung by Marguerite, Mephisto and Faust, a magnificent bunch of darkest damask roses fell at my feet, lovely for me. Of course I picked them up; terrific applause, trio repeated. When we got off, fearful scene. "Ah, mon Dieu," screamed Mephisto, jumping off both feet at once; "How dare you? dey are mine, mine, de roses; give them to me." "Oh, yours, are they?" said I, "all right, take them," and I threw the flowers at her. "Dis donc, Dick!" cried my fair Satanic friend, and flew off to the managerial sanctum sanctorum in quite the most sulphurous way.

We had Aynesly Cook for Valentine, a fine artist, with a grand voice, but always grumbling except when engaged with the chorus or seeing if the skirts of the ballet hung quite right. There is no doubt that the young ladies had a most ameliorating effect on a somewhat erratic temperament, that was never so perfectly under control as when in the presence of Mrs. Aynesly Cook.

Wagner was played by Miss Lennox Grey, just returned from India, with a mysterious brown Ayah, and lots of spangled muslins and beetles and cedar-wood boxes, and attar of roses, and no end of airs and graces. Miss Grey was the daughter of Mrs. Caulfield of the Haymarket, and sister to "Johnny" Caulfield of the Oxford. Well, she was a lovely woman, and as "a boy" created no end of a flutter in the front rows of the stalls. She wâs the first lady whistler I had ever heard, and would have run Mrs. Shaw very close indeed.

It was as the Street Arab in "Little Faust" that Miss Jennie Lee gave us a first taste of that peculiar quality which developed into the unapproachable glory of "Jo." She was dressed in fluttering silken rags, and carried a gilded besom, with which she brushed the dust from the path of our magnificent Mephisto, and her "Copper, yer 'onour! copper!" was one of the landmarks of the representation.

Then the Cabman. We had a real hansom and a real horse driven by the late Mr. C. Wilmot, of the Grand Theatre, Islington. In those days I used to regard him with much curiosity, for somebody told me he was "The Man from New Zealand." There was also a Tiger, I forget who the gentleman belonged to. He was a real smart article, very tight in the boots and hat, his small-clothes and "tops" were irreproachable, his collars and cuffs immaculate. The way he used to shoot his linen was irresistible, his nez was retroussé, and his cheek superb—so was his figure. Miss Laura Morgan portrayed with much success the peculiarities of this distinctly up-to-date young person. And there was Martha, good old Martha, played by Mr. Odell with such an air—a long and lean and sighing and languishing air.

And Marguerite: well, she was "a girl of the period," and wore all sorts of outré costumes. One was made of satin, striped, a short skirt, and so narrow you could scarcely walk; it had immense panniers. With this went a tiny hat, upon which sat upright a large squirrel, with bright shining eyes and a bushy tail. But the first dress was the traditional Gretchen of Goethe, and I much fancied myself in it. Cut à la Princesse, and fitting pretty snug, mine was, as the Americans say, like the paper on the wall. One evening while smoothing myself with both hands to remove any possible wrinkle, suddenly I felt a soft, firm hand travelling with gentle pressure from the nape of the neck down—right down my back. The sensation gave me what is called "goose's flesh." "Very nice," murmured a soothing voice.

I turned quickly, with a little shiver. The occasion was justified. I am afraid I was pleased when I found the " sensationer " was the author of " London Assurance."

But the girls, the school girls—Faust kept a Board school. I think, by-the-bye, Camille Dubois was in the chorus. She afterwards married Wyndham Stanhope, one of the sons of the then Earl of Harrington. Well, the girls, such girls, every size, sort, shape and colour, plump and petite, and blonde and brunette, cheeky and modest, forward and retiring, and all and every one of them pretty—so pretty; you should have seen and heard the school-room scene, such chatter—chatter—chatter. And what a high old time that arch impostor Faust had when we all went up to get " two slaps " for insubordination, " telling a funny story," and other iniquities. All the girls wore short frocks and pinafores tied at the shoulders with ribbons, broad sashes, and open-work socks, and baby shoes with straps. There were two prize girls, five feet ten inches in their stockings—such beauties—and we had slates and pencils, and the girls would pick off Jack, or Percy, or Bert, or Reggie in the stalls, and made some really most original studies. Well, perhaps not quite for exhibition.

Marius was Siebel. Thank goodness, I had some love scenes with him, which consoled me somewhat for my elephantine Faust. I used to think him particularly fetching when giving a falsetto rendering of "Where shall I take my Bride?" My part was really very satisfactory, I had an elopement in every act, and there were three.

Siebel turned out to be a real hero when war was declared between Germany and France. On that fateful morning we were on the stage rehearsing, and when the news got into the theatre everybody was in a state of excitement, and Marius was boiling over—wild with the desire to fight and die " pour la patrie." And, like the brave boy he was, he went to his duty—went, laden with everybody's good wishes, and his ears were deafened with the cheers of the coryphées and the chorus. Then came the terrible time, and soon it was told that Marius was lying, not with poetical propriety among the ruins of Carthage, but dead—killed outside the walls of Metz. And this broke up everybody. And his body was (metaphorically) bathed with the tears of the ballet.

But the rumour as usual was false, and he came back, which was all very well from a material point of view, but from an art point was all wrong.

When I think of " Little Faust," two occurrences always crop up in my memory. One was, that on the first night of the piece, when I made my first entrance in all the distraction of the scene, the only person I seemed to see in front (and he was at the side) was Mr. John Hollingshead; he sat in an extra stall, with his back to the stage box on the P.S., and was no more general manager of the Alhambra Music Hall, but absolute manager of the Gaiety Theatre, where they were playing "The Princess of Trebizond," with Mr. J. L. Toole, Miss Nellie Farren, and I think Miss Annie Tremaine (Mrs. George Loveday) in the cast. Mr. Hollingshead, always highly superior and sphinx-like in his demeanour, certainly on this occasion did not unbend or depart from his general habit. The other occurrence is, that one night while walking up and down at the back of the stage, waiting for my cue (a musical one), I heard some music repeated, once, twice, three times. "What's that?" said I to myself, "Some idiot keeping the stage waiting?" A scurry of feet behind me, the call-boy and Milano breathless: "Oh, for God's sake, go on, they've played your music over and over." I was the idiot.

In those days, one of our constant visitors behind the scenes was Lord Wallscourt, a charming little man, so elegant, amiable, wearing a debonair air and the most perfectly cut waistcoats, which he assured us he bought at Kino's for 10s. 6d. Leonide Leblanc was in London that season, and would often come and stand in the prompt entrance. The first time I saw her she wore a lovely black lace dress over lavender silk, and such diamonds. Amy Sheridan, too, used to come. Captain Harry Larkin was largely interested in the show, and also a little in her, I think. Poor fellow, he went to the Franco-German war, got wounded, and came back lame. One day, to my astonishment, he turned up at my house in Wood Green. We had a long and rather sad talk. He had fallen on evil days. Afterwards he went to San Francisco, and stupidly took Mrs. Muybridge on a little excursion into the country, which seemed to irritate Mr. Muybridge, for that celebrated scenic photographer (the first man, by-the-bye, to photograph the horse in action) struck the trail, and shot the gallant major, but that time, I think, "on sight," and the soft winds of the Sierras are his perpetual Requiem.

CHAPTER XI.

The Philharmonic in 1870—Mr. Charles Head, proprietor, Mr. Charles Morton, manager—The betting contingent—I make a coup—Operas in costume and twenty-five minutes —First appearance of Miss Clara Vesey—How to form a comic opera chorus—An evening party at Mr. Head's—My first view of Mr. Henry Irving—Pantomime at the East London Theatre—A Sartorial fix—A fire behind the scenes—A lesson in deportment from Mr. Isaac Cohen— The "Clodoche Quadrille" from Paris appear at the "Phil" —M. Alias—Where he came from—Whom he married —Mr. "Johnny" Gideon—His house at the Rond Point —The Alhambra closed on account of the "Colonna Quadrille"—They are engaged for the "Phil"—The apotheosis of "Wiry Sal."

In the autumn of 1870 Mr. Charles Head acquired the Philharmonic Music Hall, Islington, then known as the "Dustbin," the "Spittoon," and by other picturesque and pleasing titles. Mr. Head arranged with Mr. Charles Morton, late of the Oxford and Canterbury, to manage it, and Mr. Charles Morton considered that condensed versions of comic operas, produced and played under the direction of Miss Emily Soldene, late of the Lyceum, would be attractive, an opinion fully shared by that aspiring young person. And the run of "Little Faust" having come to an end, I was at liberty to avail myself of the offer. In a very short time the dirty old "Phil" evoluted into a bright, gay little theatre, with quite an important stage, private boxes, blue satin curtains, and a magnificent bar, extending the whole length of the corridor, with magnificent barmaids, doing a magnificent business. All the racing men flocked north to back up the "two Charlies," little tips were again procurable and lots of little fivers landed. I opened the season with a grand coup.

On the Monday before the Leger I was told to back Hawthornden. "It's all right, send two sovs. up to the Victoria Club." I took the advice—the horse was thirty-three to one—and won, and on Wednesday or Thursday, being ready money betting, I drew my merry little 66*l*. I did not see my tipster for at least six months; when we did meet I thanked him. "What do you mean?" said he; "Why, I lost 700*l*." It turned out I ought to have backed him for Tuesday, when he lost; but I, who only knew of one race, backed him for the Leger and brought it off. The gentleman who gave me the tip was Mr. Rymill.

Our first operatic venture was "Chilperic, in twenty-five minutes," condensed by Mr. W. Vandevell. Miss Charlotte Russell played Fredegonde to my Chilperic, and among the company was Mr. W. Carlton, the now well-known impressario of English opera in America, and brother to Mr. Frank Celli and Mr. Herbert Standing.

On this occasion an interesting young lady made her début, playing Brunehant. She was pretty, and had a charming figure; her stage name was Miss Clara Vesey—my sister. Mr. Morton was Clara's theatrical sponsor—and selected the name of " Vesey " from the comedy of " Money "—a not inappropriate derivation considering that she soon developed into a great personal attraction, occupying a front place in the first flight of photo'd professional beauties, and proving consequently a financial fact both to her manager and her photographer.

From the first moment of going into management—recognising the attractive force of female beauty—I surrounded myself with the best-looking and best set-up girls that could possibly be found. I selected my chorus from the ballet. The result, a minimum of voice, perhaps, but certainly a maximum of good looks and grace. Nobody ever saw my chorus still, immovable, wooden. No, they felt the music, were full of life, and, like a blooded horse, were anxious for a start. Then they understood how to "make up," which is not an accident, but an art.

During these first Philharmonic days, Mr. and Mrs. Head, on the occasion of the twenty-first birthday of "young Charley," gave an evening party at their private residence. Among the company was a distinguished-looking gentleman, of a most delightful and affable turn, who would do anything to amuse or oblige. Just when I arrived, he was giving a recitation: "And four and twenty happy boys came bounding out of school," quoth he, with a mannerism I muchly admired. "Who is it?" said I to a friend. "Don't you know?" said he. I shook my head. After a few minutes our host brought the gentleman up: "Let me introduce Mr. Irving." There was also another bright and entertaining luminary present, Mr. George Grossmith, who gave us a sketch from his "Penny Readings," and sang, "I am so volatile." Lots of professional people were among the guests: Mr. D'Oyly Carte, Mr. J. L. Toole, Fred and Harry Payne, and Mr. Addison, the father of Fanny and Carlotte; we were a very merry and representative crowd.

The "condensed" opera at the "Phil" did not come on till about 10.15, and at Christmas I had plenty of time to appear in the opening of the pantomime (for which I had been for a long time engaged) at the East London Theatre, then under the management of Mr. Morris Abrahams, who played in the pantomime too ; he had a very good voice, and we used to burlesque the grand duet from " Il Trovatore." I was the Prince, and evidently fancied myself and my costume, for every time I went to the dressing-room I looked at myself in the glass, and took an extra reef in my tights. In a moment of self-absorption I must have forgotten to button my trunks, for in the middle of the duet there went up a mighty shout of laughter. Mr. Abrahams jogged my elbow ; I looked down, and there were my trunks falling over my knees ! I stooped, grabbed them, and fled off, " never " (as I promised myself with tears of rage) " to go on again." But somebody buttoned the dreadful things up. Mr. Abrahams took me on, the people overwhelmed me with applause, and I soon forgot it. One night, in the Ballet scene, the " Islands of perpetual Delight," or words to that effect, my Princess lay sleeping on a mossy couch just about the second entrance, and I, in ecstasy, was singing " Happy be thy Dreams," when Mr. Isaac Cohen, the stage manager, came into the prompt and spoke through the symphony : " We are going to let a scene down behind you ; don't be afraid ; go on,

get an encore and sing it. It will be all right."
The scene came down in "two," and presently, from
under the canvas, trickled tiny rills of water,
running down round and under my feet. I obeyed
orders, won my encore, and sang it. The theatre
had been on fire at the back; but the discipline
was excellent, and it was got under in no time and
with no noise. During this engagement I was very
much indebted to Mr. Cohen for a lesson in deportment. As a boy I swaggered about a good
deal, generally having one foot on the P.S. and the
other on the O.P.S. "Don't do that," said he,
"Men don't walk like that, they walk like this."

Somewhere about this time we imported from
Paris for the Philharmonic a "Quadrille Excen-
trique," the famous "Clodoche Troupe." With
them, as their personal attendant, came a little
gentleman named Alias. At the conclusion of
their engagement the Clodoche party returned
to La Belle France, but M. Alias remained
in England, a captive to the charms of Miss
Price, the Philharmonic resident costumière.
They were married, and M. et Mme. Alias have
gone on costuming merrily ever since. Talking
of Paris, over from that gay city would flit every
few weeks Mr. "Johnny" Gideon, "bookmaker"
and boiler-down of effective French melodrame.

He would pop into the "Phil" on his way to Mrs. Sarah Lane and the "Brit" at Hoxton, his pockets bulging with MS., the latest sensational development at the Chatelet or Porte St. Martin —a very clever, cheery, chatty man. The last time I saw him was in Paris, in 1888, in his rooms at the Rond Point, where he lived like a prince, surrounded by objets d'art, fine tapestry, priceless mosaics, magnificent brocades, statuary, bronzes, black oak furniture, &c., &c., not the least attractive of the adjuncts being a capital wine-cellar and a capital chef.

The new "Phil" was such a success, that Mr. Morton, at the instigation of Messrs. Buckstone and Webster, was summoned twice and fined for giving stage plays without a licence. Then he applied for a theatrical licence, and got it. I suppose they subsequently buried the hatchet, for in 1871 Mr. Buckstone appeared for Mr. Morton's benefit, and later on played a regular engagement at the "Phil," and every evening after the performance "Bucky" would sit in the office sipping a little cold gin and water, and keeping us in fits of laughter with all sorts of droll stories and anecdotes. He was jolly, genial, cheerful, but rather testy and dreadfully deaf. At Islington we certainly did not allow the grass to grow under our feet. Just before we got our theatrical licence the risque number on the programme at the Alhambra was the "Colonna Quadrille," danced by Mme. Colonna, two ballerines, and a wispy slip of a girl, Sarah Wright, a pupil of Mme. Louise, a daughter of an old waiter of Mr. Morton (the little girl previously mentioned in the list of people at the Oxford). Sarah had got on since the Oxford days; Sarah was the sensation of the performance. The verb "to kick" had never been so actively conjugated before, and the Middlesex magistrates were so horrified, they took away the licence, shut up the Alhambra, and threw four hundred people out of employment. I at once engaged the "Colonna Troupe," and introduced the dance in my "condensed" opera. Subsequently the quartette was reconstructed, and we put on "The Parisian Quadrille," and boomed it with a mighty boom. Mme. Sara Bernhardt, the New Woman of that period, had just begun to shake the artistic world; so I named my première danseuse after her, "Mdlle. Sara." She was supported by Miss Gerrish, who afterwards became "the first Mme. Marius," Miss White, and Miss Lily Wilford. "Mdlle. Sara" (who had shorter skirts and longer legs than most girls), to the great delight and satisfaction of herself and all London, kicked up her agile heels a little higher than had previously been deemed possible, and was equally successful in dusting the floor with her back hair. Goodness knows what awful suffering was endured by the Middlesex magistrates, for while the Alhambra languished in outer and inner darkness, making Leicester Square a hideous, howling wilderness, filled with the sighs of the unemployed four hundred, up at the " Little Phil " in merrie Islington, safe under the shield of the Lord Chamberlain's licence, that wicked, wicked dance was danced every night. The theatre was crammed, and " Wiry Sal " was the toast of the London clubs.

CHAPTER XII.

An original burlesque, "Nightingale's Wooing," produced at the "Phil." Easter, 1871—The cast: a musical Curtius—What Sunday was made for—My first visit to Liverpool—"Chilperic" at the Prince of Wales—Mr. Mallandaine as manager and conductor—Mrs. Mallandaine as a Page—What Mrs. Kendall did not like—Mr. J. L. Toole and Mr. Justice Hawkins—Lydia Thompson on her way to America—Mr. H. B. Farnie—A new comic opera—Ordering a manager off his own stage—Mr. Downey, the photographer of Newcastle-on-Tyne—Glasgow on Sunday—What a good place it was—Mr. William Glover—The Theatre Royal—The ballet—Where it came from—At Doncaster—"The Baron" wins the Leger with Hannah.

AT Easter, 1871, the entertainment at the "Phil" was a condensed "Grand Duchess," and an original burlesque, "Nightingale's Wooing," by Frank Arlon and Arthur Rushton, the *noms de théâtre* of A. D. Dowty and John Plummer; the music, original and selected, by W. C. Levey, of Drury Lane; the scenery by Mr. Calcott, the dresses by Mr. Augustus Harris, the piece rehearsed by Mr. George Honey; P. W. Halton was the conductor, and there was a big ballet led by the Sisters

Smithers; Miss Clara Vesey played Princess Rosebud in a much abbreviated and nothing-to-speak-of skirt, but this was compensated for by the length of her train, a transparent one. Miss Hetty Tracy, of the Vaudeville Theatre, was Prince Nightingale; Mr. Levey had written a delightful ballad, to be sung by the Prince off the stage, a sort of "avant courier." At the rehearsal the Prince was physically lovely, and in those classic gems, " If ever I cease to love," and " After the opera is over" vocally perfection, but came a cropper at the ballad. Dear Mr. Levey was in despair, so much depended on the ballad. What was to be done ? " I will sing it," said I, leaping into the gulf like another Curtius, "No one will ever know." The night came, and her Serene Highness La Grande Duchesse de Gerolstein stood in her robes of state and the seclusion of the fourth entrance O.P. side and sang it. Splendid success, big encore. " Sing it again, Miss Soldene ; sing it again," said the stage manager. And I did it. " Go on," said the stage manager to the Prince, and the Prince went on, got an ovation, and stood for a solid five minutes, modestly acknowledging salvoes of applause. Next morning gushing notices; " No idea Miss So-and-so had such a lovely voice," " Sings like an artiste," " Must come off out of burlesque at once," "An artistic sacrilege that such talent should be so employed," "What is the management of a theatre about when it keeps in the dark gifts like this?" &c., &c. They set her up side of Patti. Need I say that song was "cut" after the first night?

In the summer of this year Mr. Mallandaine, musical director of the Haymarket Theatre, backed by a financier, Mr. Harry Schofield, who was young, provincial, and probably did not know any better, arranged with M. Hervé to take "Chilperic" on tour, and engaged me to travel for three months. A provincial tour in 1871 was an undertaking, an event. Careful people, especially those who had nothing to leave (except experience) drew three weeks' salary in advance and made their wills. Travelling troupes were few and far between; and Mr. Hollingshead, who always wondered what Sunday was made for, had not then discovered that the particular motive for its creation was the convenient moving of theatrical companies from one given point to another. We opened at the Prince of Wales Theatre, Liverpool, then under the management of a limited company, the only outward and visible exponents of which to our eyes were Mr. Bolt, Colonel Mum, and Mr. Tom Peers.

Mr. John Rouse was our stage manager, and played Dr. Senna. He was a cranky, cantankerous, contradicting dear old thing, full of self-satisfaction and ancient personal conceits, but a really splendid comedian—so quaint, so original, so natural. I remember one morning at rehearsal he spoke some lines in a perfectly conversational tone. The intonation caught my attentive ear as being thoroughly appropriate to that particular situation. I followed his lead. The scene at night went well, and so, without knowing, he gave me a lesson I never forgot. Miss Augusta Thompson was Fredegonde, Miss Emily Pitt Galsuinde, Mr. Alfred Bishop Nervoso. I of course played Chilperic, and Miss Clara Vesey was Brunehant.

The chorus was a capital one, and though Mr. Mallandaine, our manager and conductor, valued voices more than female physical perfection—(one would have thought his æsthetic taste should have controlled his scientific judgment, but it didn't)—still they were a showy string, with plenty of pace, Mrs. Mallandaine played the principal Page Alfred, with a song. Mrs. M. was not exactly an ideal page; like Cassio, she was lean, also, more than common tall. Nature had distinctly qualified her for petticoats, and I think it a pity to go against nature, unless in an emergency, and Mrs. Hopewell on the spot. We had a splendid band, and Mr. Mallandaine was dreadfully conscientious, and restored all the " cuts " made by the iconoclastic crew of the saucy Philharmonic. Fortunately, his idea of lengthy things in general did not extend to the skirts of the ballet, or the trunks of the pages.

While we were rehearsing in the theatre during the day, the evenings were devoted to comedy. Mr. and Mrs. Kendall were playing a season at the Prince of Wales. They were only recently married, and it was not considered good form to look at " Willie " too much, because it was understood Mrs. K. " did not like it." The production of " Chilperic " was an immense success, the chic and sparkle just suiting a cosmopolitan place like Liverpool. I think we played there for a month or five weeks. Hervé came down and fêted us, and gave a decidedly continental cachet to the affair. He treated everybody en grand seigneur, and dined us and wined us in most recherché style.

Apropos of Liverpool, Mr. McConnell, the then Revising Barrister of that city, the now chairman of the Clerkenwell Sessions, told me a capital story of Mr. J. L. Toole and Mr. Justice Hawkins. Mr. Justice Hawkins was sitting in a *cause célèbre* at the Liverpool Assizes, and Mr. Toole was playing at one of the Liverpool theatres.

The Justice sent across to say he was sitting late, and would Mr. Toole come over after the performance, and have supper with him. Mr. Toole accepted the invitation. During supper, talking over the events of the day, Mr. Justice Hawkins said he should next day "give his man fifteen years," he "deserved it." "Oh," said Toole, on leaving, "would you mind me calling at the different morning newspaper offices, and telling them about the 'fifteen years'? It will be a tip for them, and do me no end of good with the Press, exclusive information, you know, and so on." "Good God! no, sir," thundered the judge, and walked with Toole to his hotel, and tucked him up, and waited till he was fast asleep, and safe from temptation.

One night, towards the end of our engagement, Lydia Thompson, Mr. H. B. Farnie, and a large party just arrived from London were in front. They were to sail next day for America. After the performance Farnie came to my dressing-room, and said I was "the one woman he had been looking for." He had an opera bouffe that "would make our fortunes." If I would guarantee that Mr. Morton should produce it at the Philharmonic, he would not go to America, but stop in England, and prepare it for the autumn season. With the temerity of ignorance and inexperience, I promised. The opera was "Geneviève de Brabant," the first anglicised and adapted opera bouffe to make money.

After Liverpool, we went to Newcastle-on-Tyne, to the Theatre Royal, then under the management of Francis and Glover. I distinguished myself very much indeed at the first performance there. Seeing a gentleman after the first act disporting himself in the centre of the stage, and gazing with cool curiosity, not only at the girls scampering off for their "change," but also at my imperial self, I, in my severest manner, and a distinct and audible voice, said, "Tell that person no one is allowed behind the scenes, he must leave immediately," and he did. It was Mr. Francis, the manager. Such a huge joke for him! He told all Newcastle next day how I ordered him off his own stage. But we were the best of friends after.

In those benighted days the local aristocracy went to the theatre only on a Friday, and on the preceding Tuesday, if the fiat of the "Fourth Estate" were favourable, the dress circle booking-sheet would be by the afternoon all filled up. If not favourable—well, I don't know. The papers and the people were all good to me, and soon learned to look out for "Our Em'ly."

Mr. Henry Egerton, the acting manager, was a capital man of business, and a most lively and entertaining companion. He had a funny habit, when more than usually bothered, of standing on his head, "To rest his brains," said he. Poor fellow! he was lost in the fire that destroyed the Theatre Royal, Dublin, February, 1880. "Chilperic" was musically a great " go " in Newcastle, and on the first Sunday, the organist, Mr. Leggett, out of compliment, played " The Prayer" for the voluntary, and everybody said " How delightful ! " and verily it was "kept dark," and nobody revealed that it was from the wicked Opera Bouffe running at the Royal. We used to have high jinks and junketings and go for long drives over the moor and through the lovely Jesmond Dene.

It was in this city I first made the acquaintance of Mr. Downey, the photographer. Even at that remote period he was distinguished by royal patronage, and used to be sent for and stay a week at Balmoral. Mr. Downey photo'd the whole crowd and gave us lots of copies.

After Newcastle-on-Tyne, to Glasgow. The Theatre Royal impressed me as being the most gloomy place I had ever been in. I remember on my arrival seeing Mr. William Glover hard at work painting a panorama, for the "Lady of the Lake," I think. Mr. Glover was a picturesque, artistic, dark and satisfying-looking personage. He had the head of a lion, or a brigand, or a pirate, or a bushranger, or a Revivalist preacher. He would have made a lovely "Mourzouk" or "Moses," without any make up. We admired his ensemble very much indeed. When I was in Glasgow, 1883 or 1884, I got a terrible shock. Mr. Glover had shorn his leonine locks, and the imposing beard had disappeared.

Glasgow was a terrible place for the "Sawbath"-breaking, wicked, exploring and picnicing theatrical person. On Sunday, to get a carriage out of the city one had to start at 8 a.m. and walk the horses over the stones. The coaches, "machines" they called them, were "mourning" ones, funereal and dolorous; but the proprietors were kind enough to remove the feathers. Once free of the city the carriage was opened, and on you went through lovely lanes and delicious country, where the breezes blew and the birds sang and the flowers bloomed just as if it wasn't Sunday. But on the way to these delightful places one had to pass many villages, where the open windows of stone huts were full of ladies hanging out in the most astonishing state of deshabille, and whose beauty did not compensate for their lack of clothes. There is no doubt that Glasgow proper was, at this period, as proper as proper could be; but for all that one heard funny local stories, but of course not true... For instance, the "extra" girls at the Theatre Royal were exceptionally gifted with looks and exceptionally fine in physique, could move about and were well trained; a condition of things unique in those days. To explain this perfection we were told they were not ordinary "extras," but "ballet," and were always "kept on" at the theatre. Also that the Royal ballet was never recruited from outside, "They grew it on the premises."

That autumn we went to Doncaster for the race meeting, playing at the Theatre Royal. It was a most delightful jaunt—picnic, in fact. I had never been on a racecourse before—such a lovely road, such trees, such excitement, such weather, such a lovely old-fashioned hotel, such troops of friends. We went every day to the course. Every day Clara (my sister) and I asked Mr. Head for a tip, and every day he gave us a fiver instead, which we most successfully lost. What a sight it was, with the armies of people trooping along the road. Then the Leger—what a day of days! I could not keep still, but must shout loud with the loudest. I don't recollect any horse but Hannah. After the race, the Baron led her slowly along through the crush, one hand holding the bridle, the other round her neck. The people hurrahed and applauded, and when the Baron, stooping, pressed his face against her soft velvety muzzle, and kissed her, the crowd screamed with delight. And I, like the emotional idiot I was, found the tears were running down my cheeks. I could not help it. Such moments are worth *years* of ordinary things.

CHAPTER XIII.

"Geneviève de Brabant" produced at the Philharmonic, November 10th, 1871—Mr. Morton's financial faddishness —The cast—The girls—The lime-light—The rehearsals— A dress rehearsal—The sins of the costumiers—What a dress rehearsal does for the performance—Our dress rehearsal—Mr. Morton's opinion of the piece—Flight of Mr. Farnie—Production of the opera—Mr. Clement Scott's opinion of the piece—Our realistic detail—Return of Mr. Farnie.

"GENEVIÈVE DE BRABANT," Opera Bouffe, Libretto, adapted from the French by Henry Brougham Farnie, music adapted from Offenbach—e tutti quanti maestri—by ditto, ditto, ditto, produced at the Philharmonic Theatre, Islington, November 10th, 1871, under the management of Mr. Charles Morton, and the direction of Miss Emily Soldene, was the sort of success that waits upon one once in a lifetime. There was much trial and tribula- tion to be gone through before the production, and much curiosity was exhibited by the profession when it was known a new opera bouffe was on the stocks of that " out-of-the-way-place," up in the north. Many western magnates (when they thought of such an insignificant establishment at all) considered the whole proceedings an impertinence that would certainly reap the reward of its daring in utter annihilation. The opera being non-copyright, and Farnie not wishing to be anticipated or forestalled, the title was kept a profound secret, many fictitious names and wonderful and varied aliases being inscribed on the parts used for study.

In the beginning, I had great difficulty in bringing Mr. Morton up to the scratch. He jibbed, and was financially faddy. Besides, he did not like Farnie—said "Farnie and Failure" were synonymous, and added many more alliterative and aggravating arguments. But Farnie was finesseful—constant dropping wears away a stone—so ultimately matters were arranged, and the work went into rehearsal.

The following people were in the original cast: Miss Selina Dolaro played the Duchess (Geneviève); Mr. John Rouse, the Duke; Miss Clara Vesey Oswald (the Duke's pet page); Mr. Edward Marshall and M. Felix Bury, the immortal gendarmes, Graburge, and full private Pitou; Mr. J. B. Rae, the Burgomaster; Mr. Lewens, Golo; Mr. "Charley"

Norton, the Hermit; and Alfred, the potman, made a great success as the Rooster, crowing brilliantly, and disgusting all the gone-to-bed-early-chanticleers in the neighbourhood. Miss Vaughan (not Kate) played Brigette; Miss Ada Leigh, Philibert, and Miss Emily Soldene, Drogan (a pastry cook). With these artists were associated numberless and bewitching beauties, disguised as maids of honour, as pages, as citizen boys, as citizen girls, as Watteau shepherds, or as Watteau shepherdesses.

There was considerable friction and many fights among these lovely ones, each being convinced of her own peculiar fitness for (in every scene and tableau) standing at the corner of the stage, basking in the bold advertisement of the footlights, the admiring curious gaze of the public, and the occasional and furtive and fitful, and not to be relied upon, gleams of the lime-light. The lime-light in those days was an uncertain quantity, and would "fizz" and "sis—ss" and "sparkle," and "splash" and "splutter," and finally, at the critical moment, with a loud and alarming "swish," would disappear altogether.

We rehearsed the piece for six weeks, and no end of changes were made in the cast, especially in the small and "it-don't-much-matter-if-the-girl's-good-looking" parts. Mr. Farnie was most exigent in this department, and a new and handsome girl received with enthusiasm and declared by him to be the exact thing for the part to-day, would frequently (after a private interview) be pronounced by the same authority on the morrow totally unfitted for the proposed position. At last came the great, the crucial, day or night—the dress rehearsal. A dress rehearsal twenty-five years ago was a nearly unheard-of thing in England.

As a rule, the costumier brought the costumes into the theatre on the night of the first performance, at five minutes to eight, and considered you ought to be awfully obliged at their arriving at all.

Everybody's dress would be too tight in the bust and too loose in the waist, or vice versa; general confusion and disgust prevailed, and productions suffered. When the papers next morning noticed that a favourite artiste was " evidently handicapped by excessive nervousness," it would probably be an affair of hooks-and-eyes. The rages and storms, and, if it had not been for spoiling one's make up, the tears of a first night! The distracted stage manager! "Look a'ere, Mr. Smith," says the prize beauty of the theatre, by the side of whose effulgence the prima donna pales into insignificance; "Hi won't go on; wy hi'm a reg'lar sight, I ham." "You look lovely, Miss Vere de Vere," swears the diplomatic and sorely tried one. "Go on, my dear, and save the piece." The show prize girl (5ft. 11¾ins.) strolls leisurely down to the first entrance. "Why ain't you in your right place?" screams the exasperated man; "You know you go on with the King, up in four; you'll get your cue in a minute." The magnificent creature turns round slowly, her back is open five inches. "Oh, for God's sake," calls he to the rushing-about, breathless, and nearly "hout hof 'er mind" wardrobe mistress; "fasten Miss de la Chandos's dress: she'll be on in a second." The dress is inspected, and found to be so undeveloped and so deficient in details, that, though ostensibly built for the finest girl in the theatre, it is an aggravating and very open question whether it is meant to fasten in the front or the back. Then the shoes (when they arrived at all) were always damp, and so beastly short, they made one limp, or so disgustingly long, that you fell over your own toes. And the buttons, language fails when you come to the buttons, which invariably (more invariably in a "quick change") flew up to the ceiling at the mere sight of a button-hook. Mais, nous avons changé tout cela. Farnie, with his foreign ways, which were nearly all good, introduced the dress rehearsal, and the benefit to first performances cannot be overestimated.

In the first place, when you get into your costume, it fills your mind with ideas that somehow do not seem to evolute in your private dress. I am talking of the natural and impressionist school, that takes its thoughts and feelings from surrounding circumstances, and absorbs local colour and expression from its environments; not of the Delsartian and wooden cult formed on the semaphore signal basis, and the presumed entire absence of impulse and emotion.

Then, in the second place, it gives you confidence; you know your appearance is all right, you do not experience that horrid "new clothes" feeling, you have worn and gone through the part in them; the sartorial arrangements are perfect, and there is nothing to distract your mind from the exposition of your art. Our dress rehearsal was the sort of thing you can remember for a long time—a tale of woe, of disaster, of profane language, of offensive and personal remarks, of bursting buttons, and lost and misapplied and "impossible to recollect" lines, of wrong notes in the band parts, generally in the double bass and clarionet. "Good God, sir, here we've rehearsed for a fortnight, and now you find you've got a wrong note; pass over that part, Jones; no, never mind." And the conductor climbs over the musicians, and the music-stands shiver and totter on their uncertain bases, and all the parts (most of them loose sheets) fall to the ground. Then the scenery won't go right, but will go wrong, and Miss Somebody, in an access of nerves, forgets her cadenza. "Cut it out," roars Farnie, with sulphurous adjectives. "But," remonstrates the tearful girl. "Cut it out," and language unfit for Her Majesty's Drawing-room dies away at the back of the pit.

Mr. Morton sits in a front seat and severe judgment. At the end of the first act he pats his tidy little neck-tie several times, and confides to me, "There's nothing in it, simply nothing in it; utter failure. And, as for your part, why, you do nothing."

These frank expressions exactly reflect my own feelings, and no words can do justice to my depression.

The second act was even worse than the first. The band parts for my "Sleep Song" were not ready. The lime-light "medium" was wrong, and converted my Rimmels complexion into a coat of many and unbecoming colours. Everything was too dreadful. The only satisfying ones were the gendarmes, who seemed to have funny lines, and, *mirabile dictu*, knew them too.

I had a sick headache, and Mr. Morton and the distinguished adapter had a few words, after which Farnie and I adjourned to the theatre front doorstep, and he eased his mind by saying sultry and irreverent things about people in general and the management in particular. Then we two weary ones, partners in this great breakdown and unequalled frost, shook hands in dull and doleful and downcast commiseration with each other, and went our respective ways, chewing the cud of bitter and sorrowful reflections.

Next morning—it was on a Saturday, a memorable Saturday, the Saturday we all expected the Prince of Wales would die—at ten o'clock there came a messenger in hot haste, with a letter from Mr. Morton. A terrible thing had happened; Farnie had gone—fled—disappeared—packed his carpet-bag for parts unknown, leaving the disconsolate "Geneviève" to her deserved and dreadful and disgraceful fate. What was to be done? "Would I come to the theatre at once?" I went, taking my unimpaired headache with me, and found everything in a fearful confusion. During the rehearsals Mr. Farnie had conducted

Musical Recollections

everything *vivâ voce*—scenes, lights, gas, and limelight. He was gone, and there were no "plots," the men could not work. From 10.30 a.m. till 6.30 p.m. the people rehearsed, and I went through the opera with them and made out all the plots for scenes, lights, and everything.

Fortunately everybody was too much on the alert to need " calls," and that trouble was spared. But all the music cues had to be written in, and at 7 p.m. I was sitting on the floor—no, on the green baize stage cloth—cross-legged like a Turk, cross-tempered like a Turk, tired to death, voiceless, hopeless, but going to " try," if I died for it, rehearsing in a whisper the " Sleep Song."

The success of that night was a record-breaker. The enthusiasm, the applause, the crowded house! The piece went with a snap and " vim." Everybody recollected every word and made every point. The gaiety of the audience was infectious. Every line, every topical allusion was given with dash and received with shouts of laughter. How the Burgomaster blew his nose like a trumpet, " toot-ti-ti-toot-ti-ti-too," and never got any further with his speech than " In the year one." How the gendarmes sang their " We'll run 'em in," seventeen times. How everybody worked for the general good. (It is impossible to overpraise their loyalty.) How Mr. Morton came on the stage and "took it all back," and congratulated and thanked and treated everybody. How a certain gentleman, named Clement Scott, sat in the front and was good to us, and wrote a half-column notice, which, appearing next morning in the *Observer*, made a certain singer famous as Drogan, and grateful for ever. All these things live fresh and remembered in some hearts. The opera was well put on at the "Phil," everything was done very thoroughly, great attention being paid to realistic detail. Of course, as everybody has known for hundreds of years, the Duchess Geneviève's situation at a certain period in history, and also in the opera, was more interesting than correct or proper. And as an instance of the sort of carefulness that was exercised to provide a perfect ensemble, I may mention that five months after the production, Madame Selina Dolaro presented to an admiring world a girl baby, and it was called "Geneviève."

On the Monday following the eventful and never-to-be-forgotten first night, Mr. Farnie reappeared at the theatre. He had "Been to Brighton, he had read the papers. Of course he knew it would be a success, in spite of the woodenheaded management." Mr. Farnie was constitutionally shy, not to say afraid of the Press, and, when "Geneviève de Brabant" was announced, would not allow his name to appear in any advertisement or bill ; but with the second issue he had no such scruples, and gave up his incognito, as an eminently eligible thing to get away from.

The second performance was good, big house, lots of enthusiasm. H. B. F. sat in a private box, watching it from beginning to end. At the finish he came on the stage. The people flocked round, expecting a little speech, thanking them for pulling it through so splendidly. What he said was, "Everybody to-morrow morning, eleven sharp."

CHAPTER XIV.

Continued success of "Geneviève"—My picture over the prize pig pen—Visit of the Prince of Wales to the Philharmonic—Mr. Charles Morton as a connoisseur of cigars—The Islingtonites as a guard of honour—An offer to sing in "Babil and Bijou"—Return of Marius—Plays Charles Martel in the opera—A distinguished super—Our habitués—Lord Dunraven's idea of the highest form of happiness—Huddleston, Q.C., and Mrs. Broadwood—A strike in the orchestra—Sergeant Ballantine—M. Adolph Lindhcim appointed Chef d'Orchestre—What the learned Sergeant would have done " If he'd only known it sooner."

"GENEVIÈVE DE BRABANT," at the end of a year's run, was still the rage. Up to the little theatre at Islington flocked all the world, and duchesses were glad to sit in the stalls because there were no boxes for them.

The Philharmonic was the mode, both sides of the High Street were lined with carriages, and the local livery stables were filled to overflowing by the carriages of people coming from a distance. Everybody, from H.R.H. downwards, visited us. In 1872 the Prince went to the Cattle Show. Over the pen of the prize pigs hung a framed picture.

When His Highness was through with the pigs, he took in the picture. "What is that?" he inquired. "That, Sir, is the portrait of Miss Emily Soldene as Drogan, in 'Geneviève de Brabant,' now being played at the Philharmonic Theatre." "Where is the Philharmonic?" inquired the Prince. "Near the 'Angel,' your Highness." H.R.H. smiled. "A very good position indeed," said he.

A day or two after came an order from Mitchel's for a Royal box. That was a great night at the "Phil." A large box and retiring-room were especially fitted up, and Mr. Morton provided some wonderful cigars for the occasion. Mr. Morton has never smoked a pipe or cigar in his life, and consequently is considered an accomplished and cultured connoisseur of tobacco in all its forms.

His Royal Highness was treated with the greatest respect and consideration by her Majesty's lieges of Islington. When he left the theatre after the performance, the corridor was, of course, crammed, but the audience "ranged" themselves. There was no crowding, or pushing, or policemen, and a broad path was kept for the Prince by the People.

During the run of "Geneviève" I had an offer

from Mr. Dion Boucicault to play at Covent Garden in "Babil and Bijou," at 15*l.* per week, more than I was getting at the "Phil," but Mr. Morton would not release me. "Babil and Bijou" was magnificent, but financially a failure. In it Mr. Joseph Maas sang. Miss Helen Barry made her first appearance, also a great sensation. She led the army of Amazons. And I think "Spring, Spring, Beautiful Spring," was first sung in this piece.

After the Franco-German War, Marius came back to England covered with glory, but wearing his unbleached regimental shirt. He was stony broke. That did not matter. He came up to the "Phil," and I got Farnie to write him in a part—Charles Martel, with a fencing song—"Sa-ha-carte-tierce-circle, octave-prinz-quinze."

Among our "supers" at this time was a man who had immortalised himself, and in his time earned much money—G. H. Ross, the original singer of that dreadfully unpleasant and blasphemous ditty, "Sam Hall."

One astonishing circumstance about the run of "Geneviève" was that the same people came over and over again, came, in fact, every night; and at last it seemed to us folk on the stage that the opera went flat unless the usual clientèle turned up. Amongst our habitués was the late Sir James Farquharson (Piccadilly Jim). He was a little peculiar. One night, when "Sara the Kicker" was electrifying everybody, I said to him (he was standing by my side in the wing, looking very solemn), "Isn't she wonderful?" "Umph, yes," said he; "but I was thinking of her people; it must be very disagreeable to have anyone belonging to you gifted like that." Then there was Mr. Hector Tennant, Mr. (now "Lord") Gerard, Mr. (now "Sir") Horace Farquhar, and his brother, the well-known actor, Gillie Farquhar, Sir George Wombwell, Lord Gifford, Lord Rodney, Lord Mayo, just home from India, Lord St. Leonards, "Johnny" Woodhouse, diplomat, Ralph Milbanke, ditto, and lots of people that nowadays one meets in all corners of the earth, and who say, " Don't you remember? I used to come to the Philharmonic, don't you know?" Then everybody always finishes up with "Ah! those *were* jolly times." Lord John Hay was a frequent and delightful visitor; so fond of sitting in a box and criticising the girls' skirts—an inch wrong this way or that, gathers not properly distributed, or not correctly graduated, one skirt longer than the other. Nothing in that way escaped his observant and nautical eye. He explained his familiarity with his subject by saying that as a boy he always was on hand when the flannel and warm winter petticoats were made by his mother for her poor parishioners. General Fleury and his sons used to come nearly every night. The General was all right, but the sons were—well, not so all right. But, after all, our jolliest constant visitor was Lord Dunraven—gay, bright, clever, full of life ; and who after the opera would walk home with us, cut the cold beef, and open the oysters and stout with the unconventional facility of the man who has been everywhere, done everything, and who had (as he told us) found the most perfect form of happiness when lying on his back, kicking up his heels, and shouting at the top of his voice on the loftiest peak of the Rockies. Such a sportsman too. One night he offered Mr. Morton a blank cheque, to allow two of the principal ladies "a night off" for the purpose of attending the Italian Opera, on some swell and out of the common occasion. Need I say that "The Governor" put on no end of official frills, and would have nothing to do with the cheque, the proposal, or the proposer.

Handsome Huddleston, Q.C., came sometimes; not alone, but always with a duke, a marquis or an earl. He had an immense reverence and weakness for the aristocracy. I was told a funny and quite true story about him. One season at Baden, on arrival he entered his name on the hotel register " Huddleston, Q.C., London ; " immediately after him came Mrs. Broadwood, who added to his entry, making it read " Huddleston, Q.C., London, Toady, and Tufthunter." The German hotel keeper, not understanding English, had the entry printed in the *Fremden Blatt* (visitors' list) ; it went everywhere, and was a great joke for everybody—except, of course, Huddleston. Sergeant Ballantine, too, came very frequently, and one night came in the nick of time. During the troubled days of the Franco-German War, M. Lindheim, the Chef d'Orchestre of the Varieties at Paris, was staying in London on a visit to his daughter. Mr. Farnie recognising the value of such co-operation, offered him an engagement as conductor at the Philharmonic. And Mr. Blank, who had been appointed by Mr. W. C. Levey, was given a fortnight's notice. On the Saturday evening that Mr. Blank received the notice, the house was crammed. Five minutes past eight came. The artistes were on the stage, ready, waiting ; the feet of the audience began beating impatiently. Ten minutes past eight, and no orchestra in. Mr. Morton rushed down into the band-room. The band had struck. They would not enter the orchestra unless Mr. Blank's notice was recalled, unless he was reinstated, and given six months' engagement certain. It was an awful position. The audience were making themselves still more audible. Mr. Morton argued with the men in vain. They were immovable. Just then Sergeant Ballantine put in an appearance. He heard the men's demands, then said, "You persist in refusing to play for Mr. Morton to-night, unless he gives Mr. Blank a re-engagement. Is that it?" "Yes," answered they. "Very well," said the learned Sergeant, "then there is nothing else to do. Mr. Blank must have his engagement." They adjourned to the office, where an agreement was hurriedly drawn up, signed and sealed. "There, Mr. Blank," said the Sergeant, "I think that is all you require." "Thank you," said Mr. Blank, jubilantly. The band rushed into the orchestra, and all went merry as a marriage bell.

On Monday morning there was a call at eleven o'clock, for "the band with M. Lindheim." In forty hours the orchestra had been reconstructed, and not one of the men who struck or the conductor were allowed to re-enter the theatre. Mr. Sergeant Ballantine advised Mr. Morton that Mr. Blank's contract was not worth the paper it was written upon, being obtained from Mr. Morton *in terrorem*.

Ballantine was full of fun. One day, some one meeting him, said, "Well, I see Walter" (Ballantine's son) "has married a widow with lots of money." "Yes," said the learned Sergeant, "and if I'd only known it sooner, I'd have married her myself."

CHAPTER XV.

"Fleur de Lis," by Leo Delibes, produced—Mr. Head and Mr. Morton have a lawsuit—I am a witness—Mr. Fred Stanley's *bon-mot*—"Geneviève" on tour—Gaiety Theatre, Dublin, manager, John Gunn—A picnic to the "Valley of the Thrush"—A talk over the old Queen's Theatre, Dublin, and Mr. Harry Webb—A missing witch—At the Prince's, Manchester—Boston Brown and breakfast at the Queen's Hotel—Mr. Charles Calvert and my sister's boots—A Manchester "Peeping Tom"—In Edinburgh Theatre Royal—Mr. and Mrs. J. B. Howard's first season—Row by the pittites, Birmingham—Prince of Wales Theatre—With "Jimmy" Rogers—I visit the Philharmonic Theatre, Islington, London—A demonstration.

In March, 1873, "Fleur de Lis," music by Leo Delibes, book by Mr. Farnie, was produced, with not much success, but ran to the end of the season. I am sorry to say we were all so happy and fortunate that Mr. Morton and Mr. Head fell out, and a lawsuit was the result. Mr. Morton had arranged with Mr. Hollingshead to give some matinées at the Gaiety Theatre which were a great success, and quite an eye-opener after the usual "Corporal's Guard" which attended matinées in those prehistoric days. When I sang at the

Gaiety Theatre on Saturday morning, I would not sing at the Philharmonic Theatre on Saturday evening, considering one performance a day quite sufficient. Mr. Head, among other things, said such goings on injured his property. There was a trial at the Guildhall. Mr. Justice Brett was the judge. I was a witness, and had a new black velvet cloak trimmed with chinchilla, and went into the box very satisfied with myself. The counsel argued pro and con. When they got through, the judge turned to me, standing patiently in the box. " And what do *you* think, Miss Soldene ? " said he. I said I thought the performance given with such success by the Philharmonic Company at a first-class West-end house like the Gaiety was calculated to give an *esprit* to the Philharmonic. Verdict for Mr. Morton. Mr. Fred Stanley, Mr. Morton's solicitor, thought I was a very first-class witness indeed.

By-the-bye, Mr. Stanley said a good thing the other day. He had a clerk who robbed him and absconded. Talking the matter over with his son-in-law and partner, Mr. Hedderwick, Mr. Hedderwick remarked : " Did you ever hear So-and-so " (naming the culprit) " was an excellent violinist ? " " Never," replied Mr. Stanley ; " but I know he was a great fiddler."

The first tour of "Geneviève de Brabant" was a triumphal promenade. One of the most delightful places visited was the Gaiety Theatre, Dublin. John Gunn was the manager. He made no end of a fuss with us, and was particularly pleasant and complimentary to me, saying I " Was such a good finisher and always left off with a bit in hand." The audience were always demonstrative, and on the first night, after any number of calls, I had to sing my favourite song, " The Minstrel Boy."

There was an old woman who sold apples under the gateway near the stage door. When I came out she insisted on shaking hands with me. " Och, the blessin' of God and th' blessed Vergin be on you," says she. "Sure you've got Irish blood in yer heart, or you cudn't sing 'Th' Minstrel B'y' like that."

On the Sunday we were there we had a lovely outing. Mr. John gave the boys and girls a picnic up in the Wicklow Mountains, in "The Valley of the Thrush." Handsome Michael Gunn was just then back from Italy, and the ladies found him no end of an acquisition. I drove with old Mrs. Gunn in a mourning coach, drawn by two thin black horses, with excessively long, but thin, tails. When the path was very steep they jibbed and went sideways, and wanted to turn round and go back. I would if I had been they. We had dinner at the Monastery, and got lovely "praties" boiled in their jackets, which were brought smoking and steaming in an iron pot by two young monks, the most picturesque things in religion I had ever seen; they were very tall and straight, and wore a grave expression, and black serge gowns tied with a rope. They had bare sandalled feet and such eyes. The Superior being away, we went into his cell to take off our bonnets. It was all cold and stony and dark, with a little window high up in the wall, through which the sun never crept. We were dreadfully wicked, and sat upon the good man's bed, and shook up his bolster, *such* a hard one.

During our stay in Dublin, a party of us went over the old Queen's Theatre, and Mr. Edward Marshall, one of our "gendarmes," was full of anecdotes of when he, as a young man, played an engagement under the management of Mr. Harry Webb (of Two Dromios' fame). At the back of the stage ran the roadway of a livery mews, and in those days, when they required realistic effects, as, for instance, in the "Courier of Lyons," the stage was thrown open and the roadway utilised for real coaches and horses. Mr. Harry Webb was at once manager, actor, acting manager, and money taker, and equally energetic in all these departments. One night (the bill was "Macbeth"), during a lull at the receipt of custom, he ran up, and peeped through the bull's-eye window of the centre boxes to have a look at the "Witches Scene." Horror! he could only see two witches. Rushing round to the stage, he shouted, "Where's the third witch? Where the h—l's the third witch? Fine him, fine him." ".You're the third witch, sir," replied the stage manager. Mr. Marshall was the "first witch" and Mrs. Harrington "the second." During that season "The Tempest" was produced, with Mrs. German Reed (Priscilla Horton) as Ariel, Mr. Marshall as Trinculo, and Mr. Harry Webb as Caliban. " I have never seen anyone approach him in that part," said Mr. Marshall. Mr. Webb was also very fond of playing the "Courier of Lyons," and in 1861 appeared at the Theatre Royal, Manchester, in the dual rôle of Dubosc and Lesurques, supported by a young actor named Henry Irving.

In Manchester we played at the Prince's. That was in "Boston Brown's" time. We breakfasted with him at the Queen's Hotel; such a breakfast, real American; lobsters, and lots of fruit, steaks and fried oysters, hot rolls and corn bread, tea, coffee, and iced water, hot cakes and molasses. Mr. Calvert was the Shakesperian manager, and looked upon opera bouffers with a severe, not to say a cold and critical eye. That was in the morning; but in the evening, when I went off my first exit, I saw him examining with much interest the fashion of Miss Vesey's (the pet Page) boots. She wore them particularly high, and had one foot on a stool, so he could make sure, exactly, how they were trimmed. When he saw me, he murmured something about he "had not noticed anything precisely like that before." Up to this day I am not certain whether he meant the boot or the wearer.

During our stay in Manchester I had a little adventure with a local "Peeping Tom." My dressing-room was down stairs, and next it was the carpenter's shop or stores. One night, having sent my dresser out, I was alone drawing on my tights, when I had the strange feeling that every-one has felt, the feeling that there is someone in the room, or that someone is looking at you. I turned round, the room was empty, but the impression remained. The dressing-table was a plain deal one, about two feet wide, and extending the whole length of the room. On it were no fallals or frills, simply a toilet cover, and between the table and the floor the space was open. As I sat in front of the glass, "making up," the impression was repeated more strongly than before. I pushed my chair back, and in doing so looked beneath the table, where, immediately opposite to me, in the dark shadow, my eye encountered another eye. I could not actually see, but I knew, I felt it. I finished dressing, and when going out turned down the gas. Then, after a few minutes, we opened the door cautiously, and from a hole in the skirting-board came a faint gleam of light.

When I was changing for the second act, the man was caught on the other side of the wooden partition, with his eye glued to a gimlet hole. I need not say he was kicked out of the theatre there and then. He was an old hand, and, in the course of years, had probably acquired more knowledge than he knew what to do with.

I had a similar experience in Denver, Col., U.S.A. One night I got the same feeling, and, looking up, saw the face of a gigantic negro in a space left between the wooden shutter of the window and the ceiling. He also was caught, and enjoyed the soundest thrashing he'd had for a long time.

In Edinburgh we played at the Theatre

Royal, Mr. and Mrs. J. B. Howard's first summer season of management. Our arrival had been much anticipated, and many stalls had been filched from the pit, and when the doors were opened there was a rush of pittites, who jumped the claim, and sat in the seats they had been accustomed to. There was much hubbub, but things soon quieted down. We did great business, and Mr. and Mrs. Howard always told people I was their "Mascot," and set them going in their first venture.

We had splendid houses at Glasgow, Newcastle-on-Tyne, and Liverpool, also at Birmingham, where we played at the Prince of Wales's, manager, Mr. "Jimmy" Rogers. The first Saturday night we were there, the local stage manager said, "If there's any disturbance, shall I let down the curtain?" "Let down the curtain," said I; "What for?" "Well, Saturday nights there's generally a bit of a row. Last week, Miss Holt's burlesque company were here. They threw cabbages and carrots, and we had to lower the drop." "Well, you won't send down the curtain, except at the proper time, while I'm here," said I, "and they won't throw cabbages and carrots to-night." And they didn't. I must say though I felt rather surprised to see the whole gallery in its shirt-sleeves, cuddling big bottles of beer.

We did an enormous business in Birmingham. People used to stand for hours waiting for the doors to be opened, and blocking the street. But they were a bit scandalised at "Sara."

I have since been told that "advance booking" had never been indulged in at the Prince of Wales's till the advent of the "Geneviève de Brabant" company.

When I returned to London, Mr. Head, who was now running the Philharmonic on his own account, had just produced "Madame Angot," with Miss Julia Mathews as Lange, and Miss Selina Dolaro as Clairette. I had a box booked, and, accompanied by Mr. Morton, Mr. Hollingshead, and party, visited the theatre I considered I had created. I went to see the opera, not to occasion a demonstration. But a demonstration took place that stopped the performance. Directly the audience caught sight of me they commenced to cheer, and before they would be quiet I had to bow from the box, like H.R.H., or any other great swell, and I found it very nice indeed. It is a legend (why, I don't know) that I am the original Lange, in English, but it is not so. That distinction, if it is any, belongs to Miss Julia Mathews.

Musical Recollections 135

CHAPTER XVI.

Production of "Mme. Angot" at the Gaiety Theatre, November 1873—The cast—The dress rehearsal—A baby (a Royal baby) show in the Green-room—My benefit—The fog that killed the bullocks—Mr. Morton's benefit—Mme. Desclauzes and the baggage man—Mr. "Levey" Lawson—Moore, the stage-door keeper—People who came behind at the Gaiety—"Mme. Angot" at the Opera Comique in 1874—Inauguration of the 10s. 6d. stall—Visit of their Royal Highnesses the Prince and Princess of Wales—Visit of the Prince Imperial—A Violet night—The first man in Coomassie.

"LA FILLE I E MADAME ANGOT," music by Charles Lecocq, book adapted from the French by H. B. Farnie, was produced at the Gaiety Theatre, November, 1873, under the joint management of Messrs. John Hollingshead and Charles Morton, with the following cast:—

Ange Pitou	Mr. E. D. Beverly.
Larivaudière	Mr. R. Temple.
Louchard	Mr. E. Marshall.
Pomponnet	Mr. F. Bury.
Trenitz	Mr. J. G. Taylor.
Amaranthe	Mrs. Leigh.
Estelle	Miss Ewell.
Hersilie	Miss Clara Vesey.
Clairette	Miss Annie Sinclair.
Mdlle. Lange	Miss Emily Soldene.

In the Conspirators' Chorus was Mr. Ludwig, the now celebrated bass, and Mr. George Appleby, since principal tenor in the American Opera Company, "The Bostonians." The last time I saw him was in Buffalo, U.S.A. He was playing José to the "Carmen" of Miss Zelie de Lusan.

I was nearly out of "Mme. Angot," I did not like playing Mdlle. Lange. But the management was persuasive, and, as it turned out, the part suited me, and I made both reputation and money out of it. We rehearsed and produced the opera in one week, playing "Geneviève de Brabant" every evening. On the first performance, I only got my verse of the "Quarrelling Duett" as I came off the second act. I learnt it while changing for the third, and remembered it all right. Miss Annie Sinclair was a charming Clairette, the opera went splendidly, and even Meyer Lutz complimented us.

At the dress rehearsal there was a terrible sensation. Moustachios not being admissible in conjunction with white wigs, the gentlemen of the chorus were directed to shave. Much affliction and great resistance resulted from this autocratic order. There were many prize specimens of moustachios in the company, military and magnificent. But the costumier, Mr. A.

Harris (father of Sir Augustus), and the management were firm, the hirsute appendages sacrificed, and the artistic unities preserved. All the feminine belongings of the male chorus resented this desecration dreadfully, and Mrs. Quinton, my wardrobe mistress, whose husband was super-master, also a fine-looking man, and had to "go on," came to me with tears in her eyes: "I'd rather throw up the engagement," said she, "than my William should lose his moustachios."

One day, when we were rehearsing, there was a great fuss and rushing about, and giggling of the girls. Somebody said, "There was a Baby Show in the Green-room, sixpence admission, and with the money the stage hands were to drink the baby's health." "What baby?" said I, "and why sixpence?" "Oh my, Miss Soldene; what, don't you know? why, it's a Royal baby." "Royal rubbish," said I. "It's true," said little Miss Brown, "I know all about it, Lardy told me. Why, it's the Duke of—" "Miss Brown called," shouted call boy. Miss Brown flew, and the secret is still unrevealed, at least, unrevealed by Miss Brown.

At the end of the season, Messrs. Hollingshead and Morton kindly placed the theatre at my disposal for a matinée. Fortunately for me, the house was sold out before the day, for at the performance the theatre was filled, not with people, but with fog, the fog that killed the cattle at the show that year.

Mr. Morton also had a benefit at the Gaiety, on which occasion the celebrated Mme. Desclauzes, the Parisian Mdlle. Lange, appeared. Madame was a remarkably fine, handsome woman, very tall and perfectly proportioned. I placed my dressing-room at her disposal, the one on the stage, the window of which looked out over the stage door into Wellington Street.

After the performance I went in to have a little chat with her. She was sitting in front of the toilet table, in a very negligé costume, wearing in fact only one garment of a delicious and delicate fineness, profusely trimmed with lace. Under the table stood a tin box containing her stage costume. A knock at the door. I opened it. The baggage man for the box. "Entrez, entrez," said Desclauzes. "Mais, Madame," said I, pointing to her limited lingerie. "Ce m'est egal, entrez." The man shuffled in. "Là!" and, shoving back her chair, she pointed to the box with her two bare, pretty pink feet.

One of the nicest men I ever met within a theatre was Mr. Lionel Lawson, most kind, genial and even-tempered, the best and most stimulating of audiences, and to hear that "Lawson's in his box," was the signal for everybody to put their best leg first, though being all so good, it was difficult to discover the best. Nothing bothered him but disagreeables and discussions.

One day I was, I am afraid, rather inclined to fight over some question. "My dear child," said he, "take the theatre and all that is in it, but don't get angry." His sudden death was a great loss to all who had ever had the good fortune to be associated with him.

My recollections of the Gaiety would not be complete if I did not remember Moore, the stage-door keeper, who died suddenly and alone, one Sunday, while at his post. Mr. Hollingshead told me there was no reason for him to be there on a Sunday, but no persuasion could keep him away. He evidently thought the theatre would come to grief or disappear if he were not there. Moore was not at all a modern Cerberus, for while attending strictly to his duties, he had a polite answer to every question, and to charge his memory with a particular message did not necessarily cost half a sovereign. The stage entrance to the Gaiety was different in those days, and one had to go down several steps to his sanctum sanctorum, decorated with pretty pictures of the pretty chorus and ballet girls, and his favourite artistes. He died while I was abroad, but the news brought him back to my mind so vividly, sitting in his chair, bending over the fire, rubbing his hands, and turning round with a pleasant smile: " Oh, yes, he's up in his offis. The guv'nor 'ull always see you, miss."

Not many people came behind at the Gaiety, but among them were : The Marquis of Blandford, Lord Rosebery, Lord Macduff, the Marquis of Anglesea, Mr. (now Sir) Douglas Straight, Lord Alfred Paget, Lord Dudley, Lord Londesborough, Sir George Wombwell, Sir James Farquharson, and the Posnos.

After the Gaiety season we went to the Prince's, Manchester. "Mme. Angot" was non-copyright, and already three companies had invaded Cottonopolis, but Cottonopolis did not respond. We had been billed a month ahead. The public waited for us, and a magnificent business was the result. At Christmas, 1873, Messrs. Morton and Hollingshead rented from Lord Dunraven the Opera Comique, and put on "Mme. Angot" there. The business was enormous. During this time the 10s. 6d. stall was inaugurated, and booked weeks and weeks in advance. Miss Patty Laverne had replaced Miss Annie Sinclair as Clairette, and was without doubt (up to that time) the best English representative of the character.

The Princess of Wales, as every one knows, is a very placid great lady, especially at the theatre; and while H.R.H. would, leaning on the front of the box, enjoy the play and lead the applause, the princess presided in severe rigid, decorous, and unmoved dignity. The only time I ever saw her laugh was at the "Quarrelling Duett" in the third act of "Angot." Bending slightly forward, Her Royal Highness regarded the pugilistic ladies at first with curiosity, then, finally appreciating the situation, sank back in her chair laughing and applauding heartily, and nodding to the Prince as if in approbation. That night we sang the duet four times.

The first place of amusement the late Prince Imperial visited after the death of the Emperor was the Opera Comique. When I heard His Imperial Highness was coming, I bought up all the violets in Covent Garden Market, and decorated the Prince's box. It was a bower of violets, and every member of the company—band included—wore a bouquet of violets.

"Mme. Angot" is full of dreadful republican sentiments, and I hated to repeat them before the prince, so young, so unfortunate; such a nice face too, oval, distinguished, rather melancholy, with beautiful eyes, like his beautiful mother.

Not the least pleasant episode about February, 1874, was getting the news that Lord Gifford, one of "the boys" at the Philharmonic, who had gone out to Ashantee, was the first man in Coomassie.

In the summer of this year we went another provincial tour.

CHAPTER XVII.

Practical Mr. Bateman—My season at the Lyceum—"The Grand Duchess"—Miss Clara Vesey as Wanda—Revival of "La Fille de Mme. Angot"—Mme. Selina Dolaro as Clairette—A little contretemps—A remembrance of Captain Burton, the African traveller, and Mr. Holms, the spiritualist—Our engagement at Portsmouth—Our sea experiences—What the youngest Home Ruler in the House of Commons said.

BEING under contract to go to America in the following October, I thought I should like a two months' London season previous to starting. The Lyceum was advertised to let. I wrote to Mr. Bateman. He wanted 90*l*. per week. Well, of course, the rent of a theatre is only a small part of the expenses, and it seemed an immense responsibility to assume, so I played about and fiddled and faddled, and was altogether uncertain and undecided. This was in the pre-syndicate days, and taking a theatre was a serious matter. However, one evening practical Mr. Bateman appeared at my lodgings in Birmingham, where I was then playing, and talked to me in so exceedingly practical a fashion, that when he drove me down to the theatre he carried in his waistcoat pocket my cheque for 300*l*., the first month's rent in advance. It was decided to produce the "Grand Duchess," and we did so in splendid style. Mr. Jolly, of the "Fantasies Parisiens," Brussels (who had made such a great impression the previous year in London by his performance in "Girofle Girofla," "Je vous presente un Père," &c.), was engaged at 60*l*. per week to put it on the stage. Mme. Auguste (Mrs. A. Harris) made the costumes, which were exceedingly correct and exceedingly elegant. My dresses were magnificent, and my train of embroidered pale-green satin was a veritable antique, and had belonged to the Empress Josephine. Everything was very lavish, and my sister, Miss Clara Vesey, covered herself with glory and the "Jeunesse Dorée" of that period with enthusiasm by her performance of Wanda. And when Mr. Beverly, as Fritz, sang "D—— the regulations," and kissed Clara full on the mouth and the stage, there was a fearful flutter and movement in at least the four front rows of the stalls, and Mr. Beverly was considered to be an envied and enviable fellow for some considerable time. Personally I had a great success as the Duchess. My voice was in capital order, my appearance suited the character, and my acting was pronounced equal, if not superior, to all previous Duchesses of Gerolstein. But strange to say, and I don't mind recording it now, I never cared for the part. All the kind and good notices and praise I received was as dust and ashes in my mouth. I never believed in myself; I never got (as the foreigners say) " dans le peau " of the rôle, and, in spite of pleasing my critics, failed to please my own inner consciousness. We got an exceedingly good month's business out of the Duchess, and arranged for the second month a revival of " La Fille de Mme. Angot." By this time Mme. Selina Dolaro was an artiste of importance, and I, wishing to give every *éclat* to these farewell performances, engaged her at a large salary to sing " Clairette," and out came the " ad." :

"Miss Emily Soldene has much pleasure in announcing she has secured the valuable assistance of

MME. SELINA DOLARO,
who will appear in her original character of
CLAIRETTE
in
' MME. ANGOT.' "

Then there was a little contretemps. As a

matter of fact the concluding verse of the Opera belongs to Clairette, and she ought to sing it. But I, having the might instead of the right, I suppose, had always appropriated it to myself, and brought down the curtain with me in the centre of the stage *en tableau,* as is the wont of *prime donne* in power to do on every possible occasion. When we came to rehearse the scene, Mme. Dolaro positively refused to appear unless she sang the rôle as it stood in the score. Of course she was perfectly right, and, as for me, I can only say "mea culpa."

The upshot of this was that next morning the "ad." said:

"Miss Emily Soldene begs to announce that in consequence of a misunderstanding

MME. SELINA DOLARO

will *not* appear in her original character of

CLAIRETTE

in

'MME. ANGOT.'"

That afternoon a neat little coupé bowled up to the Lyceum stage door, a neat little tiger threw open the carriage door, and a neat little lady stepped into the theatre and made a neat little speech, and "was so sorry to upset the arrangements," &c., and next morning the "ad." said :

"Miss Emily Soldene has much pleasure in announcing that, the misunderstanding having been arranged,

MME. SELINA DOLARO
will appear in her original character of
CLAIRETTE
in
'MME. ANGOT.'"

Such lots of notable people came to see us during these two months to say "bon voyage" and "au revoir!" Among them two stand out in my memory, strongly, distinctly. One, Captain Burton, the African traveller, tall, dark, bronzed, masterful, and much addicted to long conversations with the ladies of the ballet and the pages. I, an untravelled one, with the bump of veneration largely developed, regarded him with the greatest awe, admiration and respect. Still, I could not get away from the fact that he was artistically made up; the cheeks rouged a little and the eyes Indian-inked a lot, just as if he were going on the stage.

The other was Mr. Holms, the spiritualist. Thin, fair, fragile, with beautiful, soft, silky, wavy pale hair, long delicate hands, æsthetic in appearance and charming in manners. People used to say he had been in the inmost confidence of the late Emperor Napoleon, and was still so with the Czar of All the Russias. This gave him much mysterious interest in my eyes.

The very last engagement we played before leaving England was at Portsmouth. Our business was so big, that one night a whole boat-load of people in full dress from Ryde had to return home disappointed. Their seats not having been booked in advance, when they arrived at the theatre there were none available. At Portsmouth we commenced our sea education. A friend of ours brought round his steam yacht, and every day, wet or fine, rough or smooth, we used to go a-yachting to get ourselves familiar with the sea and all its nasty ways. We were dreadfully afraid of crossing the Atlantic, not thinking of danger, but of being sick. One very stormy day we crossed to Ryde, got drenched in the yacht, and dried in the hotel, returning through a high sea and a thick, cold, drifting mist. We were close to Southsea, when a huge shadow fell across the boat. Looking up, we saw an immense vessel. It was the troopship *Serapis*, coming out slowly, but with a way on her. For a moment it seemed we must go under. But a voice on our little craft was heard, loud and clear. "Shove her along like h—ll!" sang out the youngest Home Ruler in the then House of Commons. These explicit directions were obeyed, and we were safe. But it was a close shave.

CHAPTER XVIII.

We sail for New York October, 1874—Mr. Morton leaves his umbrella behind—Queenstown, the lovely—The perfume of the ship—The clergy—The weather—A gentleman's opinion of the ship—The donkey engine—The donkey lady—The wreck—The gallant captain who changed his shirt at sea.

HAVING previously made our wills, increased our life insurance, and sunk no end of capital in the accident insurance, the Soldene Opera Bouffe Company, under contract to Messrs. Maurice Grau and Carlo Chizzola of New York, started for the United States by the good ship *Celtic* (White Star Line), under the command of Captain Kennedy. Of course such a voyage was not to be without incident, the first thrilling event being the discovery that Mr. Morton had left his umbrella behind. I had the Captain's cabin on deck. Speaking from experience, deck cabins on ocean voyages are a mistake. Everything on this, my first sea journey, appeared to me novel and wonderful. The big ship was very full, and we had at least half a dozen of the clergy on board. At this period I was not aware that their presence settled the question of the weather for the trip. But it did.

When we steamed into Queenstown, we were enchanted with the lovely view—the soft green hills fading into the distance, the pretty white houses clustering and climbing up their grassy-terraced sides. Such a busy scene, such a bustle, such a rush, such a lot of babies, such a tearing and a howling; boats coming off with nice Irish emigrants, like the song; boats coming off with nasty Irish emigrants, not at all like the song. Bawling old apple-women, smoking short black pipes, rolled up in voluminous shawls, with a profound belief in the superior excellence of their recently polished and rosy-cheeked apples; "Broths of b'ys" who sold ancient newspapers, and fled with the price before the date was discovered. Such shouting and swearing and rushing, such weeping, such shrieks and whistles from the engine, such sudden gusts of explosive and impatient steam, such squeaks from circling flocks of sea-gulls. And, oh, goodness gracious! when we stopped, such a smell, horrid! made up of pea-soup, burning rancid oil, and hundreds of other indescribable abominations. I asked a gentleman what could possibly produce such results. "*Multum in parvo,* madame," said he, with solemnity; "*multum in parvo,*" and I wished such a disagreeable thing had never been invented.

Up to this the weather and my digestive organs had behaved beautifully, but no sooner had we turned "first to the right" out of Queenstown, than the sea went up (the ship with it), the sky came down. And this performance being repeated *ad lib.,* I retired to my cabin, a dead thing, or words to that effect. What horrors! what suffering! Ah! if the ship would only be still for five minutes! Neither the ship nor anything else would be quiet for five minutes. All the company were prostrate, and my sister Clara soon dangerously so. The wind for days blew and howled. The sea ran after us in high mountains, and catching us up, fell on the deck in great floods. The sky was grey and the clouds rushed along in dark gusty masses.

Every now and then the ship took a header, then sprang up with a sickening bound, skimmed the tops of the waves like a swallow, shook, shivered, vibrated, and, shaking the water from her shining sides, down she went again. In a moment of confidence a gentleman kindly informed me she would certainly "break her back one of these days." There seemed no peace, no quiet, and the donkey-engine at night was dreadful—rattling, groaning, heaving, hissing, banging. But sometimes I forgot my miseries, lying in the dark, listening to the song of the sailors—a nice tune, with lots of "ahoys" and things I could not understand. But I heard that one of the passengers denounced it as improper—something about a "waist" or a "stays" or a "knee"—and his wife desired that this particular ditty should be discontinued.

After a day or two some of the girls crawled on deck. They were dilapidated, but in spite of that were attended assiduously by the officers of the ship—Dr. Neale and Purser Harbord. The male passengers, too, were most kind, and insisted upon dividing their arduous duties with the official departments. Somehow the lady passengers did not seem to share this anxiety.

One morning, endeavouring to look through my port, I found it blocked by the broad back of one of the clergy (they were from France bound for Canada). Peeping over his shoulder, I saw he was reading a book—"A French and English Conversation." His reverence was diligently studying the language of the "Coulisse."

About the fifth day we sighted a small ship—a wreck. Instantly all was bustle and excitement. Away went my *mal de mer*. I flew out on deck. Yes, there she was, not very far off—a little French brig, no sails, only a rag flying, no masts, nothing but a hulk, and one of our boats already pulling to her help. The sea was dreadfully high, but we could plainly see—a white flag flying? No, it was the captain drawing over his head a clean white shirt, to receive our officer in a manner worthy of the politest nation on earth. The little ship was the *Molièr*, of Marseilles, out goodness knows how many days from New York.

The captain, who was also the owner, would not abandon her. On board was all he cared for in the world—his wife, his boy, his dog, his cargo, and his crew of six. Our captain sent out what he asked for—provisions, oil, masts, spars and sails.

As we steamed quickly, swiftly away, all hands mustered on deck, and gave one great cheer for the brave captain, his brave wife, his boy, his dog, his cargo, and his crew of six. And then we women watched (as well as we were able through our falling tears)—watched the little black tossing hulk, outlined against the grey and cold and cruel sky, watched her disappear down over the horizon, into the dark night—into the pitiless solitude of the raging, hungry sea. But she " got there all the same," paid for all she had, and sent a present for the captain. This news we heard months after in Philadelphia.

CHAPTER XIX.

A New York fog—The New York air—The New York roads—The New York Hotel coach—The American lady of 1874—The American lady of 1896—Oysters and champagne at Delmonico's—Fourteenth Street in 1874—The Fifth Avenue Hotel—A five days' bill—The cockney sparrows in New York—The New York theatres and their managers in 1874—The "Soldene" boom—Our first appearance—Harry Montague—Dion Boucicault and George Rignold in New York—Where the married ladies went—Where the unmarried ladies went—Where the men went—Press opinions.

ENTERING New York harbour, we ran into a thick white fog, also, as nearly as possible, into a fishing boat. For a few minutes there was much rushing about, fog horns blowing, and steam whistling, but fortunately for the poor fishermen, we just missed them. We were all very much astonished at the fog. We had been told by Americans, and they ought to know, there was no fog in America, only in England. The first thing that struck me on landing was the delightful air—brisk, sharp, exhilarating, invigorating. The second thing that struck me (badly, too) was the roads, made of big stones and bigger holes. The carriage bumped and bumped, worse than the ship. In those "arks upon wheels," the public coaches, sent down from the principal hotels, the passengers had to be strapped to the seats to keep them from being hurled out like bolts from a catapult. The streets were gay with painted advertisements, hung overhead upon stretched wires. The ladies were most extravagantly dressed for the street, wearing long bright-coloured silk, brocade, and moiré skirts, dragging on the ground, from under which trailed in the dust dainty white petticoats, that somehow suggested Leicester Square. The American lady of 1874 was of an entirely different physique to the American lady of 1896. She was fragile, more than fragile, painfully thin, with tiny hands carried affectedly in front of her (like the performing poodle carries his fore paws when travelling on his hind legs), tiny feet, flat feet, and no instep. She was made up to an alarming extent, not only her face but her figure. Those were the days of the Princesse robe, and the New York *elégante*, a thin, wiry, contourless being, by the aid of a wash-leather combination, padded and shaped from the neck to the ancle, appeared a thing of beauty, if not a joy for ever. The ladies of New York were aristocratic in features, delicate and refined, with beautiful eyes, fine hair, fine teeth (when not their own). They wore diamonds at the breakfast table, and cut through the vast space of the hotel dining-room with elevated, thin, nasal, metallic voices, that made one's skin creep. They lived on huge underdone "porterhouse" steaks, roast beef "rare," ice-creams, iced water, candies, hot cakes, and molasses. They never drank anything strong, except in the seclusion of their sleeping apartments, and then, with the intelligence of the ostrich, they stood the empty bottles outside the door. They were always chilly, passing their days in rocking chairs, with their feet well up to the stove, and could not venture into the overheated corridors of the hotel without a small shawl over their shivering shoulders. They had a bad habit of looking strange people over from head to foot, and back again, and making audible remarks. "Mais nous avons changé tout cela," and now there is no more delightful person on earth, than the plump and athletic, swimming, boating, batting, golfing, riding, climbing, bykeing, tailor-clad, trainant-voiced, cultivated, cultured, American lady of to-day. In making these remarks after this long period of time, I am justified. These ladies in those days used to call us beefy Britishers. Of course, at the time we could not retaliate, but some women can wait.

The first thing I had to eat in New York was at Delmonico's in 14th Street, oysters and champagne. Fourteenth Street was smart then, and no stores disturbed its aristocratic calm. We put up at the Fifth Avenue Hotel, which was rather expensive, and our first bill 255 dollars for five days and three persons.

On our way "up town," we heard the cheep, cheep, cheep, of the cockney sparrow, specially imported to exterminate the American caterpillar, which had a nasty weakness for dropping off the trees, and down one's back. The sparrows were luxuriously lodged in little wooden boxes nailed to the trees. We found New York quite Parisian in aspect and gaiety. The principal theatres were: Booth's, under the management of Palmer and Jarrett; Wallack's, manager Mr. J. Wallack; the Lyceum, managers Messrs. Grau and Chizzola, and Union Square, manager—I forget. The most-talked-of beauties of the stage were Miss Fanny Davenport and Miss Bessie Sudlow. My first evening in New York was passed at the Union Square. They played "The Hunchback," in which Miss Clara Morris, the Bernhardt of America, and Mr. Stuart Robson appeared.

We opened at the Lyceum Theatre, 14th Street.

about the second week in November, 1874, and, in spite of our "beefiness," caught on. Soon everything "Soldene" was the rage: "Soldene" shoes, "Soldene" stockings, "Soldene" hats, "Soldene" gloves, "Soldene" fans, "Soldene" coiffure. But the greatest sensation was the "Soldene" girl. Never had been seen such girls, real girls, with fine limbs, complexions nearly all their own, beautiful creamy (Maintenon) white skins, figures perfect, gay, bright, healthy, laughing girls, blonde girls, blonde girls with blue eyes, with demure dreamy grey eyes, soft brown eyes, bright hazel eyes, but they all had black lashes. Then their hair, wonderful hair, running the professional long-haired sisters very closely indeed—yellow, flaxen, red, bronzy, long, wavy, crispy, curling and rippling. I don't think the *colour* of the hair was warranted, and I don't think people expected it. "The Boys" simply went crazy over this crowd of imported loveliness.

Our first opera was "Geneviève de Brabant," with the following cast:—

Drogan	Emily Soldene.
Geneviève	Agnes Lyndhurst.
Brigitte	Lizzy Robson.
Cocorico	John Wallace.
Oswald	Laura Carthew.
Golo	H. Lewens.
The Burgomaster	J. B. Rae.

Charles Martel	E. Laurant.
Philibert	Miss E. St. Clair.
Grabuge	Edward Marshall.
Pitou	E. D. Beverly.
The Hermit	C. Gibbons.
Pip	Miss Nichols.
Peterkin	Una Brooke.

Maids of Honour.

Christine	Marie Williams.
Gudule	Ruth Reid.
Isoline	Laura Carthew.
Gretchen	Helen Travers.
Faroline	Beaumont.
Gertrude	Julia Roberts.
Houlbionne	Jessie Loftus.
Yolande	Nellie Reid.
Brandamante	Clara Gray.

Musketeers of the Guards: Messrs. Maynard, Cullen, Cooper, Quine, Hillier, Quinton and Cottrell.
Members of Council, apprentice cooks, citizens of Curacao: Misses Rose Roberts, Kate Chorley, &c.

The conductor was Mr. George Richardson, a nice man, but dreadfully bilious, especially at rehearsal, hurrying over each number at a dreadful pace, and catching on to each cue with a sharp "Next." When anything went wrong, he invariably remarked, "What 'er yer a doin' of?" I afterwards heard that he made much money, buying and selling public-houses, which, of course, must have interfered somewhat with his artistic instincts.

We had a splendid reception. The Press spoke of us in the most delightful terms. I was found to be "magnificent," magnetic (I am afraid they also said " massive "), possessing " vim," a grand voice, and, better than all, knew what to do with it. The vocalisation of the other principals, also the chorus, was " good." The comedians were not too funny, just funny enough. The dresses were " out of sight," and the whole show was pronounced " real elegant." But after all it was the "female youth and beauty" that fetched them. All the critics found these " indescribable," "irresistible." During the season we produced " Chilperic," " La Fille de Mme. Angot," " La Grande Duchesse," and " Mme. l'Archiduc," which had just appeared in Paris. A friend of M. Chizzola's brought over a vocal score, and in one week it was translated, scored, studied, learnt, rehearsed, and produced.

While we were in New York, Mr. Dion Boucicault, at Wallack's Theatre, produced and played " The Shaughran," first time on any stage. Mr. Harry Montague appeared as the English officer. At the same time, Mr. George Rignold was playing at Booth's Theatre, " Henry the Fourth," with great success. The married and middle-aged ladies of New York worshipped at the Rignold shrine. The young and unmarried ladies bowed down before the æsthetic beauty of Montague, and haunted Mora's galleries, absorbed in the photographed presentment of the artist. They stood two deep on doorsteps and stools to catch a glimpse of him on the Broadway. It was a Montague delirium. Both these gentlemen drew crowded houses—all feminine, no men. Why? Because all the men had gone to the Soldene show.

Though not as a rule approving of the exhibition of testimonials, I think I may with propriety insert the following, one charm of it being, as the gentleman said on the steamer, " *Multum in parvo.*"

The Play, New York, November 10th, 1874.

"SOLDENE ENGLISH OPERA BOUFFE.

" The brightest anticipations in respect of the immediate and marked success of the Soldene English Opera Bouffe Company have been realised. Miss Soldene and her artists have won a victory of which the results are destined to be enduring, and English Opera Bouffe, thanks to their complete, artistic and effective interpretation, is now accepted as a standard amusement. Monday's performance at once established this form of entertainment in the foremost rank of representations of the period. The rendering of ' Geneviève de Brabant ' is well fitted to swiftly secure so desirable an end. It combines the fun of Opera Bouffe with the elegant wit of English comedy; the lyric beauty of Italian Opera with the tunefulness and dash of Burletta music; the comicalities of satire with the splendour of spectacle. So rare a grouping of excellences in one entertainment is seldom, if ever, brought about, and as a consequence, the immediate decision of the French 'nerve' of the acting, the charm and beauty of the singing, and the magnificence of the stage costume, was of the most favourable kind. Under these circumstances it is almost unnecessary to say that the programme with which the season of Opera Bouffe at the Lyceum Theatre was so felicitously inaugurated, is to be retained throughout this week. 'Geneviève de Brabant,' with its melodious songs, its rattling finales, its wealth of drollery—a most important element of which is the 'Gendarmes Duet,' greeted invariably with a delight which finds expression in half a dozen encores—remains upon the bills until 'The Daughter of Madame Angot' is in readiness. Meanwhile, although everybody in New York seems likely to form an opinion, from personal impressions, of the Soldene English Opera Bouffe Company and its achievements, it may be mentioned here that the Metropolitan Press has given voice to its views, and clothed them in words of which there is no mistaking the force. The *Tribune* speaks of the new attraction at the Lyceum Theatre as a simple and charming amusement, placed amidst artistic and refined conditions, within the reach of the public. The *Herald* remarks that ' Nothing approaching to the completeness of the mise-en-scene has been witnessed.' The *Times* says: ' So vivacious, bright, and inoffensive an entertainment is rarely offered.' The *Sun* observes that the ' company far surpasses all former ones in point of musical accomplishment.' We might quote additional phrases of similar import, did not crowded houses and enthusiastic applause prove, nightly, that the high character of English Opera Bouffe and the perfection of its recital by Miss Soldene and her artists are already understood and appreciated."

CHAPTER XX.

My sister's illness—A successful hypnotic suggestion—We say things we don't mean—So do the Americans—A collar-making colonel—At the Metropolitan Hotel—The bullets that killed Jim Fisk- At the Belvedere Hotel—In the rooms of Parepa Rosa—Parepa's wonderful success—Parepa's wonderful appetite—The farewell of Charlotte Cushman—At Booth's Theatre - New Year's Day in New York—Arrival of Stephen Fisk from England.

In the midst of the rush, hurry and worry of the first appearances, there came to me a terrible fear. My sister, who had been so ill on the ship (so ill that she had to be carried ashore), instead of getting better on land got worse, and soon developed gastric fever. She was exceedingly weak and low, and the fear that possessed me was the fear that she would die. At last came a crisis, with continued insomnia. The doctors tried everything; the more sleeping draughts the less sleep; there she lay awake, always wide-awake. Then came the expressed opinion that if she did not get sleep, her recovery was very uncertain.

In these days of "Trilby" fads, "hypnotic

suggestion," &c., &c., I think the record and outcome of my successful experience may prove interesting.

I knew nothing of animal magnetism, or scientific theories of any kind. The impulse and power that came to me, came from the love and affection I bore her. The night the doctors had given me such serious news I came back from the theatre tired, weary, worn out with anxiety. I took some supper, sat down quietly and read a little, in fact rested and recuperated myself, mind and body. Then going to bed, I lay down beside my sister, and, taking her in my arms, held her close and petted and patted her like a baby, and "hushed" her, and prayed in my heart, as I had never prayed before, that she might sleep. And after a bit she dozed for five minutes, then woke up wondering, "where was she?" "Hush," said I, sharply, "Go to sleep," and she did; slept for six hours. When she awoke I was exhausted, stiff, cramped, all the strength had gone out of me, I could not move, but she was saved. From that night she got better, and in about three weeks appeared, looking lean and rather like a young stork, but safe. We heard subsequently that the very night of my experiment, "Death of Miss Clara Vesey" had been cabled to England.

Socially there were lots of things in New York to amuse us Britishers. The dreadful disgraces we got into by using English expressions that to American ears conveyed all sorts of things we did not mean! Then some American locutions and customs more than surprised us. One day a gentleman called at the hotel. I informed him that he could not see Clara : she was out. Presently he electrified me. " How long has your sister been on the street? " said he. Then a charming person was introduced to us, a Colonel Somebody. He made several calls, had a box at the theatre, and sent flowers, &c., and he was an exceedingly nice man. After a few days the "Colonel" came to say " good-bye." " Would we allow him to send us each a little present as a remembrance of a very pleasant time?" We were " delighted." In due course the present arrived; two boxes full of " collars," " cuffs," and " dickeys." Our Colonel was a wholesale collar manufacturer of Troy, N.Y. We changed our hotel twice during our stay in New York, going first to the Central, where I had a suite of rooms, in one of which James Fisk died, when he was shot by Edward Stokes in 1872. To these rooms there was a private stair ; and in the wall on the left-hand side as you went up could still be seen the bullet marks. We finally settled down at the Hotel Belvedere, Fourteenth Street and Fourth Avenue.

The general sitting-room was full of portraits of artists of all countries who had come to America, and the proprietor was full of anecdote. The rooms I had were occupied by Mme. Parepa Rosa when she first went to America, where she created an immense furore and made much money. Mr. Wehrle told me how nervous she was before she appeared, and how she sat in " that chair " sewing the bows on the dress she was to make her début in. " Ah," said he, " madame never sewed her own bows on any more, somebody else did it." He told me she had a lovely disposition, and a wonderful appetite. She would eat a chicken before she went to her concert, and two when she came back.

About this time there was a great sensation in the art world. Charlotte Cushman was about to retire. " Her farewell appearance " was to take place at Booth's Theatre. All the city was up in arms; all the great people, the mayor, the head of the police, the chief of the fire-brigade. There was to be a parade of all the societies in the city, torchlight processions, flowers, flags, bands, cannons, bells ringing, &c. Miss Cushman was to play Meg Merrilies. Mr. Howard Glover had told me in England of Miss Cushman's " Meg," her wonderful performance, her appearance, realistic and frightful, her hands and arms alone taking her an hour and a half to " make up." And when she was finished, nothing quite so terrible as this terrible "Meg" had ever been seen.

I am afraid I was disappointed. I suppose I had expected too much; but anyway, she looked and was a very dreadful old woman indeed. After the performance, Miss Cushman received the Profession on the stage, and took leave of the public. What a scene! The vast theatre was crammed; every box was decorated with flags (American), palms and flowers. The people raved and roared themselves hoarse. The band played " Hail, Columbia," and the whole audience stood up and sang it. All the ladies of the New York Theatres carried baskets of flowers, which they laid at the feet of this idol of many years. Everybody was trembling, shaking with emotion, tears were plentiful, and in that vast assembly there was but one person unshaken, unmoved—that one was Charlotte Cushman. She walked down the centre of the stage, down the flower-strewn path—an imposing, majestic figure—clad in a plain dark dress, with plain collar and cuffs, her grey hair drawn back in plain bands. She stood firm, composed, not a tremor. " Ladies, gentlemen, and the public," said she ; then, going close to the footlights, extended her right hand, and clenching it tightly as if holding something very precious, her eyes blazed out with the triumph of possession, and in a tone the exultation of which it is impossible to convey in words, she said, "My Public," "*My* Public ! "

New Year's Day used to be great business in New York. All the ladies stayed in and received the gentlemen ; everybody went everywhere, and everybody was "so glad" to see them. On the big tables stood bowls of punch, cake, sandwiches, pie and fruits of all kinds. All the men one knew brought all the men they knew, and people got pretty lively by the evening.

I received, of course; and the great surprise of the first day of 1875 to me, was—the call of Mr. Stephen Fisk, "just arrived from England."

CHAPTER XXI.

No lime-light men outside of New York—The city of brotherly love—Precept and practice—Dry-cupped by a barber—Brooklyn and its miseries—The opera ball at the Academy of Music, New York—Globe Theatre, Boston, and the Harvard students—At Ford's Theatre, Washington—Visit to General Robert Lee's old home—Baltimore mules—Buffalo—Niagara, 10° below zero—A Canadian B. and S.—" God save the Queen "—Chicago, remains of the great fire—Clarke Street, Chicago—Louisville—The " Equal Rights " Law in operation—St. Louis—" Yours merrily, John R. Rogers "—A catarrh—Going to Galveston —Tom Ochiltree—The fighting sheriff of Texas—Sail for New Orleans—The captain's musical box—The niggers—The ladies—The babies—The races and the gambling houses of the Crescent City—Why the ghost did not walk—We sail for England.

I MUST say here that America at that time was rather behind in the lime-light business, and when we left New York we had to take our lime-light man with us.

From New York we went to Philadelphia. We stayed at the Continental Hotel, and played at Mrs. Drew's Theatre.

The cold was intense, and after one night I was down with incipient pneumonia. Mr. Morton went for a doctor, and, in this stronghold of brotherly love, was hours before he could get one. They would "not attend any person connected with the theatre." At last he returned with the greatest in the city, Professor Pancoast. The treatment was heroic, very. I was cupped—dry-cupped—by a barber. I felt I had tumbled back into past centuries. The Professor pulled me through though, and in two days I was able to sing. From Philadelphia we went to Brooklyn. There was no famous Brooklyn Bridge then, and, living in New York, one had to cross the ferry every night to the theatre—cross in a carriage, of course, which drove bodily on to the ferry boat. The cold, the ice, and the snow were dreadful. The ferry boats crunching and crashing through miniature icebergs, and the stamping of the startled horses, gave us no inconsiderable amount of fright, and the theatre—the "Academy of Music"—was a great, gloomy, barn of a place. The streets, half lit, were piled up with dirty snow, and the side walks were one sheet of slippery ice. When I arrived, I found my dresser, Mrs. Quinton, had fallen down and broken her arm, but, having had it set, was waiting to dress me! I always thought people with broken bones went to bed right away; but not she. She was at once one of the smallest and pluckiest women in the world.

At this time, Madame Aimée, the French Opera Bouffe prima donna, was due in New York. The "Aimée" and the "Soldene" companies were both under the same management, "Grau and Chizzola"; so said management resolved to give a grand ball at the Academy of Music, New York, at which it was announced that Mme. Aimée and Miss Emily Soldene would receive their friends. The affair was an immense success; the tickets were 5 dols., and the receipts over 5000 dols. The ball proved interesting to me, for there I met Mr. Charles Thorne, the well-known actor, a handsome man, a charming artist, and an impertinent person, but his was impertinence that could be forgiven. He, it will be remembered, in conjunction with Mr. Stuart Robson, came over to the Gaiety Theatre and played in Dion Boucicault's "Led Astray." The cast included the late Miss Amy Roselle (Mrs. Arthur Dacre) and Miss Helen Barry. The play bills used to read so funnily: "Miss Helen Barry 'Led Astray' every night by Dion Boucicault."

After Brooklyn, we visited the principal cities of the States. In Boston, beautiful, bald-headed

Boston, we played at the Globe Theatre, and the great Harvard University supplied us with supers. The up-to-date students thereof bribed the real supers with dollars to get out of the theatre, and filled their places. One night they assisted in the performances; the next, in faultless evening dress, they occupied the front rows of the fauteuils, their places on the stage being taken by another contingent.

On our last night the whole college turned out, and they set up a barrel of beer in the Greenroom for the chorus. Never was such a scandal. Afterwards we heard dreadful stories of "rustication" and other terrible penalties.

At Washington we played in Ford's Theatre, where President Lincoln was shot; and on a snowy day we crossed the Potomac to General Robert Lee's beautiful home, confiscated to the State, in whose gardens and grounds lie, taking their rest, 24,000 American soldiers, "Union" and "Confederate." To Baltimore, where our train was drawn through the streets from one depôt to another by sixty mules, driven by mounted men with long stock whips, blowing horns, where we sampled the sort of oysters talked about by Charles Dickens, and where we had chicken, "Maryland style," and found it delicious. To

Buffalo, where in the evening the streets were dark, dismal, deserted, and we looked vainly for "Buffalo gals comin' out to-night—out to-night," &c., and while there we of course visited Niagara on a Sunday, with the glass ten degrees below zero. There was an ice bridge over the river, and a tall cone-shaped ice mountain one hundred feet high, made of the spray which froze as it flew, and hiding behind the fleecy mist were hundreds of rainbows—laughing, dancing, iridescent rainbows. Columns of ice glittered in the sun, and every branch of every tree was hung with strings of flashing diamonds.

There was no wind, and though the cold was intense, we did not feel it. We drove across the iron bridge (the toll for the carriage, if I mistake not, being six dollars) into Canada, sang "God save the Queen," and drank many S.'s and B.'s at "25 cents" each. A brandy and soda in the "States" costs you 50 cents.

Cincinnati was a wonderful place. They "boarded" the car horses upstairs on the second floor, and the dears hung their heads out of the windows to get a little fresh air, and to see what was going on below; they only wanted a pipe in their mouths to make the picture perfect. And when we walked home from the theatre at night, the rats, as big as kittens, ran down the grain-choked gutters in squeaking crowds.

At Chicago we played in a horrid theatre, at the wrong side of the city, the "Academy of Music." There we had great business, and very nearly a tragedy. One of the girls poisoned herself for the love of Mr. J. B. Rae, the "Burgomaster." But a stomach-pump and much admonition averted a fatal result.

In 1875 Chicago bore many traces of the great fire of 1871. Whole streets were in ruins, and tall, gaunt trees, burned and black and cindering, stood along the lake front and on each side of every thoroughfare. I went to a lake-side cemetery, three miles from town, and all the way there walked on the charred remains of the wooden sidewalk. We found the granite tombs with their plate glass tops melted and fused (the granite and glass together), lying around in huge confused heaps. The melted stone had run along in streams like lava. One of the sights of Chicago at that time was Clarke Street: all Dime museums, Dives restaurants and gambling saloons.

We visited one of the Museums, saw the Fat Lady, and the Living Skeleton, who was going to marry (up in a balloon) the belle of the city; the man who fasted for a fortnight; the man who won the great wager by eating two quails every day for a month (I am told this feat is impossible); a Mormon who arrived one morning with six wives—six wives being against the city ordinance, they locked him up, and when he got out of jail, the Dime proprietor gave him (and the wives) a big engagement; the boy who lived on nails (tenpenny ones preferred). There were two Aztec idiots, with long, squeezed-up heads and tiny faces, who jabbered and spat upon and polished a tin can all day. The girl made a rush at every man and wanted to kiss him; we were afraid the boy might be troubled with a similar complaint, so retired.

When we got to Louisville, the law conferring on coloured people equal rights with white people had just come into operation. Previously to this, no coloured person could ride in the same car or eat in the same restaurant with a white person; no coloured person could take a room in any hotel. In the theatre coloured people had to sit in the place (a top gallery) set apart for them. All this was now to be changed, and white Louisville was in a ferment of fury and rage. Dreadful trouble was expected. There was a rumour that some coloured men were coming into the "Parquet" (stalls), and the white gentlemen

Musical Recollections

swore that if they did they'd shoot them "on sight." The trouble came one evening—I was on the stage—two fine-looking, well-built, coloured men in evening dress walked down the aisle, when, up rose the white men, and covering them with their revolvers, said one word, " Git." They went, and there was no shooting till they got to the street, but we had no more coloured men in the stalls.

At St. Louis we played at the Olympic Theatre, where, " yours merrily, John Rogers," as he has since told me, had his ears boxed for looking at the Soldene girls instead of attending to his business, which was that of selling programmes. In the second week of this engagement I was down with unmitigated American catarrh, an inflammation of the soft bones of the head, attended with fever and ague ; a horrible complaint ; but, in spite of three doctors, I did not die—no, I was carried into the train, and we started for Galveston.

When we left St. Louis, the streets on each side were banked up with walls of dirty snow at least ten feet high. We turned our faces due south, and in twenty-four hours were among the flowering peach trees, miles and miles of them, warm summer sun and roses. Straight on we flew over the balmy scented plains; and at night out came the fire-flies in millions, the voice of the bull-frog was heard in the land, and my catarrh disappeared as if by magic. Over more plains, where wild horsemen were rounding up and lassoing live cattle, and busy buzzards were picking out the eyes of dead ones; on into the land of the orange, magnolia and myrtle. The commissariat had to be carried on board the train. There were no dining-cars tacked on in those days—a thousand miles and no refreshment bar! Think of that, ye shades of "Shorts." The girls got lots of fun out of the cooking; they had little alcohol stoves, and sausage-frying, tea-making, spluttering fires and unparliamentary language went on from early morn till dewy eve.

We came to Houston, Texas, just as the sun was rising; the pretty town was bathed in gold and rosy pink. Houston was fast asleep, except for a lot of yawning, grinning niggers, and flocks of black birds with yellow beaks.

Here we had breakfast—a fawn-coloured steak, about as thick as the sole of one's boot, and resembling it in more ways than the thickness; a sweet cake to eat with it, muddy coffee, condensed milk and a Chinese paper serviette. Off again, past lots of places, and lots of loafing Texan men, tall, nearly too tall, with long legs, graceful figures, dark blue eyes, black hair, and big slouch hats—sombreros, I suppose.

At last we came to Galveston and gazed upon the sea. How delightful to feel the soft, warm ocean breeze! Harry Greenwall, the manager of the theatre, did all in his power to make us happy and comfortable, and succeeded, even to having "14" painted on the door of my room in the hotel, when he by chance heard I was superstitious about "13." The theatre was not exactly Drury Lane, and stinging nettles grew up close to the stage door. The public was pleased with us. The Press, rather chaste and faddy, found us "improper," which we were not, also "beefy," which perhaps we were; everybody can't be as fat as a stoat nailed on a barn door. Anyway, every night the theatre was crowded. We had a real good time, beautiful drives on the beautiful beach, and saw wonderful things and people, not the least wonderful being the famous Tom Ochiltree, the fighting sheriff of Texas, now a New York dude, and the, as nearly as possible, successor of Ward McAllister. He told us stories, and everybody knows what steep stories Tom Ochiltree can tell. On the last day of our stay we had an early matinée, twelve o'clock noon, and afterwards, escorted by the mayor, the citizens and the city band, went down to the wharf and took the steamer for New Orleans. They gave us a splendid send off, and the last thing I recollect of Galveston is that as we steamed out into the Gulf of Mexico, the band (all brass) struck up " God save the Queen" in five different keys, one for each instrument. Our voyage was monotonous—all deadly sick. Mr. Morton, going to get me a cup of tea, never came back, and after some hours was discovered in the scuppers wet through, prostrate, collapsed, his hat spoilt, doubled up. He always went on a voyage in a frock coat and a tall silk hat. My sister and I had the captain's cabin. The captain was very polite. It was a big room, and when the ship rolled and you didn't like that, you could lie one way; and when she pitched and you didn't like that, you could lie the other way. The captain had a musical-box, and when we had a more than common attack he came in and wound it up to "amuse us.'

We got into New Orleans at 7.30 Sunday evening, and at eight were on the stage. We opened with "Geneviève," at Ben de Bar's Theatre. The house was packed, the audience enthusiastic. We stayed at the St. Charles Hotel.

New Orleans is a lovely city, oranges growing in

the front garden, the sun always shining, the sea always glittering. We saw everything, including alligators, and the races. All the jockeys were coloured boys. The big ones wore the little ones' clothes, and the little ones wore the big ones' clothes. The coloured people in New Orleans are not only first-rate servants, they are first-rate entertainers. One morning at the hotel, my boy, leaning over my shoulder, said, "Yours berry bang-up costume las' night, missie. I jes' like ter git dat ar pattern. Ise goin' ter play a lady myself—der Lady ob der Camillas—at der club nex' week."

I had two women to wait in my dressing-room, both as black as the ace of spades. When anything went wrong, or was lost, one in the absence of the other would shake her head and say, "Not me, missie, der *dark* gal did it." Then, if my "wash" did not arrive in time they would be in a fearful state, and make remarks not at all flattering to their sister help. "Dem dam yaller trash, dey jes' goes aroun' in der madame's clothes, den dey wash 'em up an' bring 'em back ter de hotel—late." The expression "goin' aroun'" involves possibilities which one does not care to contemplate in association with one's own lingerie. I asked a bright-eyed black and laughing wench which she liked best, these times or the old ones. She showed all her white teeth, an' guessed "she like de ole times best—berry nasty missie, but berry nice massa." These people are passionately fond of dress and flowers, and my women decked themselves in the roses sent to my room, and powdered and rouged their faces, and looking in the glass, "Yah yah'd" themselves nearly into hysterics with delight.

We had ten performances a week, playing every evening, including Sunday, and three matinées commencing at noon. Siesta at 3 p.m. The theatre at the matinée was always a picture—such lots of children, most extravagantly and beautifully dressed. Nearly all the New Orleans ladies at this time were in deepest mourning, and those that were not wore black; lovely ladies, too —beautiful, graceful. They brought heaps of flowers and threw them on the stage *à la Anglais*.

The city of New Orleans is full of gambling dens, open to the street, and people gamble there all day and all night. One day an awful thing happened. The "ghost did not walk." Somebody (old enough to know better) on his way to the theatre to pay salaries, went into one of these places with the dollars, but came out without them.

In May, 1875, we sailed from New York for England, and on the voyage I made a friendship that has lasted ever since—Miss Annie Wood, of New York, the well-known actress, being kindness itself. My sister and I were very ill, and Miss Wood was the nicest and most practical Samaritan I ever met.

CHAPTER XXII.

"Fleur de Thé"—Miss Bessie Sudlow at the Criterion—Mr. James Mortimer of the *Figaro*, howled at by the gallery—Mr. D'Oyly Carte's dilemma—Miss Bessie at Manchester—My season at the Park Theatre—My benefit—Lady Gregory's opinion of Opera Bouffe—A visit to Paris—People met there—Miss Kate Monroe's pretty feet—Production of "Mme. l'Archiduc" at the Opera Comique—Miss Kate Santley—Our aristocratic *clientèle*—An *embarras de richesse* of Dukes—Mr. Frederick Clay—"Trial by Jury," with Miss Clara Vesey as the Plaintiff.

IN 1876, at the Criterion Theatre, under the management of Mr. D'Oyly Carte, was produced a new comic opera, called "Fleur de Thé." I went to the first performance, curious to see Miss Bessie Sudlow, of whom I had heard so much in New York. Those were the days when the gallery howled at Mr. James Mortimer of the *Figaro* every time he entered a theatre. They howled that night, but did not disturb the equanimity of James, who, turning his back to the stage, took through his opera glasses a prolonged and very exhaustive survey of his tormentors. When the gods had finished with him, they turned their attention to me. "Hall right, Em'ly, we're a cummin a Saturday night," alluding to my forthcoming engagement at the Park Theatre. Miss Bessie Sudlow, as " Cæsarine," made an immediate success under peculiar and adverse circumstances. It seems the Lord Chamberlain at the last moment objected to the original cast, and said unless a certain character was cast differently the piece could not be played. Mr. D'Oyly Carte, in agony, wired Mr. Michael Gunn of Dublin. Mr. Michael Gunn sent on Miss Sudlow. She studied the part in twenty-four hours, played it in boots damp from Davis, in dresses that had to be pinned on her. She sang songs she did not know to tunes she had never heard, wedded to words improvised as she went along. But she was all right, "pulled through," as she says, by "that dear Goossens," the conductor. When the notices came out, Miss Bessie Sudlow found herself famous; she had captured the town. Miss Sudlow was a capital hand at playing parts on the shortest notice, and at Manchester repeated as nearly as possible the "Criterion" coup. She was travelling with Mr. Carte's company, and the opera was "Mme. Angot." Miss Patty Laverne, Clairette; Miss Selina Dolaro, Lange. At rehearsal these ladies disagreed as to the *tempi* of the duet, " Happy days of childhood." Dolly wanted it one way, Patty wanted it another. The end of it was Miss Dolaro refused to play. More agonies for Mr. Carte. He rushed off to the lodgings, Mrs. Brown's, Ducie Street, Oxford Road—(Dear dear, what a lot of us recollect Mrs. Brown, and Charlotte, good old Charlotte)—where Mr. and Mrs. Carte, Miss Bessie Sudlow, and Miss Haidee Crofton were staying. " My God, Bessie," said he, bursting in, " you'll have to play Lange Monday night." " Why, I'd never seen Lange, except you one night at the Lyceum, before you went to the States," said she to me, when telling the tale. Well, she had the clothes pinned on. Still she " got there " all the same, received an ovation from her audience, and a diamond bracelet from Boston Brown. Then, as all the world knows, not long after she played the most important part of her life, and became Mrs. " Mike " Gunn.

The season at the Park Theatre, under the management of Parravicini and Corbyn, was a success. We woke up the Camden Town people with " Chilperic," and in the Pages' chorus was Miss Maud Branscombe, the most photographed young person of the period. Kate Paradise and her troupe danced ; Mdlle. Sara and her troupe danced.

At the conclusion of the engagement I took a benefit, at which the late Lady Gregory (Mrs. Stirling) appeared. I held a great reception in the Green-room, and she regretted she had not come in contact with Opera Bouffe before. She had "no idea we had such a good time." For that night "Trial by Jury" was sent up from the Royalty. Rose Stella sang the Plaintiff (originally played by Miss Nellie Bromley). Fred Sullivan was the Judge, and Mr. Penley the Foreman of the Jury.

Some little time after, my sister and I went to Paris to see an opera of Hervé's, called "Poulet et Poulette," in which Schneider appeared. On arriving at the theatre, the Varieties, I think, the first person we saw was a gentleman we knew, a Scotch gentleman, who was then only "a Peer," but who is now "a personage." "How long shall you stay here?" asked I. "God knows," said he; "I never leave home more than twenty-four hours without getting a telegram to come back immediately: 'One of my sisters bolted.'"

Miss Kate Munroe was in a box that night, looking particularly pretty. A box in a French theatre is too awful—stuffy, hot, no room to move. Miss Munroe had the smallest feet (with the exception of Mrs. Judge Russell's, of New York) I had ever seen. "Why, Kitty," said I, "give the boys a treat and yourself a little comfort; hang your toes outside, instead of keeping them inside this band-box."

When I returned to London I arranged with Mr. Morton to go to the Opera Comique, to play Marietta in "Mme. l'Archiduc." Miss Kate Santley was engaged for Fortunato, and though people prophesied we should not get on together, we did, excellently, and sometimes talked over the "Bell goes a-ringing for Sarah," and "Up the Alma's height" days at the Oxford.

Our regular *clientèle* this season was much more aristocratic than it had ever been: The Duke of this, and His Grace of that. The late Duke of Sutherland was very fond of coming, and times out of number we, from the stage, would see the audience a wee bit agitated, and His Grace disappearing in a flurry, "fetched to a fire." The late Duke of Newcastle occupied one particular stall every evening during the entire season. Dukes, with us, were remarkably plentiful, and one of our principal ladies could not eat her dinner unless her particular duke cut it up. Dr. Lennox Brown was our throat specialist. For myself, I did not need professional attendance. But he made it up to me by sketching pretty pictures on the walls of my dressing-room. Mr. Frederick Clay, the composer, a most charming person, came very frequently; he wore very fetching open-work shirt-fronts, with coloured silk beneath, one night pink, another night blue. Sir George Armitage, too, dear old man; like poverty, he was always with us. "Mme. l'Archiduc" did not "catch on" to the amount expected. The real success of this short season was "Trial by Jury," in which Miss Clara Vescy sang the Plaintiff with much distinction.

CHAPTER XXIII.

Return visit to America, October, 1876—"Trial by Jury"—A sensation in Boston—Booked for Brooklyn—Get Kate Claxton to take the date—The Brooklyn Fire, December 5th, 1876—Loss of 326 lives—H. M. Stanley—How history is manufactured—Kate Claxton—The "Fire Queen"—The *Chicago Times* finds my mouth too large—Shaking hands with "Sitting Bull"—My principal tenor's notorious wife—San Francisco—Dr. Cornelius Hertz—At home—A visit to Chinatown—Chinese Johnnies—Dr. Hertz makes a present—A 1250 dollars seal-skin jacket—Mr. and Mrs. J. C. Williamson, in "Struck Oil"—Maggie Moore— "Jimmy" Moore's pants—Début of Mme. Modjeska— Robbery of the Modjeska diamonds—A Chinese weapon —Sail for Australia July, 1877—The Southern Cross— Auckland, New Zealand—Miles Paget—Where the Maori ladies carry their husbands' pipes—Auckland oysters— Where the hens sleep—Sail for Australia—My sister as a poker-player—We land in Sydney, New South Wales, September, 1877.

AT the end of October, 1876, the Soldene Opera Bouffe Company, under the management of Mr. Chizzola, sailed again for the States. On November 19th we opened in Boston at the Globe Theatre, playing "Mme. l'Archiduc" and "Trial by Jury" to an immense house.

"Trial by Jury" was a sensation in Boston,

where it had been previously played by the Alice Oates Company, but made no particular impression; no pains being taken with the presentation, no mise-en-scene, and none of Mr. Gilbert's "business." We gave it, with the scenery, costumes and effects, as in London, and this burlesque of British institutions (burlesque, which afterwards found fuller expression in H.M.S. *Pinafore*) caught on with the Americans to an unprecedented extent. Boston simply went wild, and every night "Trial by Jury" was played twice, every number being encored and repeated. What havoc the bridesmaids created! and there was a movement all over the house when the fair Plaintiff appeared. The cast was: The Defendant, Mr. Knight Aston; Counsel for the Plaintiff, Mr. C. Campbell; the Judge, Mr. J. Wallace; Usher, Mr. Dalton, and the Plaintiff, Miss Clara Vesey.

On Monday, December 5th, 1876, a memorable date, we were due at the Brooklyn Theatre. I did not wish to play in Brooklyn; I hated the place. So Mr. Chizzola got Miss Kate Claxton, who was then travelling with the "Two Orphans," to fill the date, and we went to Providence, Rhode Island. How well I remember seeing the announcement next morning: "Brooklyn Theatre burned, seven lives lost." That seemed horrible enough, but the number went up every hour, till it reached the frightful total of 326. It was too terrible. Of course the excitement was intense, but everything in America is on a large scale, and life and death there are not regarded as a matter of so much importance.

Some years ago, at the time Mr. H. M. Stanley was elected Member for North Lambeth, I came across an anecdote told by an American editor. "It was the night of the great Brooklyn Theatre fire," said he; "myself, three reporters and Stanley, who was a special reporter, were coming home from the fire, hurrying through the crowds and each getting ready to get in his share of copy for the first edition. 'I will treat of the street scenes, the present condition of the fire and the estimated loss,' I said to one of the reporters, 'and you tell the incidents of the fire.' To another I said, 'write of the origin,' to the other, 'get a list of the burned-out people. We shall get our copy together quicker in that way.'

"Stanley had shifted away as I was speaking. 'You can count me out,' he snapped in his peculiar hound-like way. 'You are going to write that all have escaped from the fire. I know better. I am going back to explore the hot ruins. There are ten people killed if there was a stick burned.'

"Back he went on a keen run, and next morning my newspaper had the distinction of being the first one to proclaim a death list of what was the greatest loss of life ever known in a fire in New York State."

This is how H. M. Stanley looked at that time : " A tall, lean young man with a strong face. Dark hair set on a good rounding forehead, and the clearest pair of keen blue eyes shone under heavy brows."

I told you everything was on a large scale in the States. At the time mentioned by this gentleman in this very circumstantial account, Mr. Stanley was in the middle of Africa, busily engaged in identifying the "Lualaba" with the "Congo" River, which he afterwards reported had an uninterrupted course of 1400 miles! Stanley disappeared into Africa from August, 1876, to August, 1877.

For months during that tour by some mysterious chance Kate Claxton and I continued close together, and wherever she went, "Fire! Fire!" was the cry. They called her the "Fire Queen," and we got afraid of her.

We broke our journey also at Chicago, playing a fortnight in Haveley's Theatre to great business. During this engagement, the *Chicago Times* came out one morning with a column about my mouth. My mouth was so big, they thought it would take "two men to kiss me." That night I had great fun and an immense fan. I was playing the "Grand Duchess." Every time I had anything to say or sing, I said or sang it, then up over my mouth went this large fan. The people soon caught on, and the opera went with screams of laughter from beginning to end. There was a nice article in another paper the next morning, saying, if I had a large mouth, I had also a good temper.

While staying in Chicago the proprietor of the Palmer House, then recently built (and the "barber's shop" of which is paved with silver dollars), asked me, would I like to see "Sitting Bull and his chiefs," who were then on their way from the Black Hills reservation to Washington, to ask their Great Father, the President, to turn the gold-hunting white man out of their (the Indian) country. The Indian warriors were on the top floor of the hotel, in a suite of rooms entirely destitute of furniture. When we entered we saw thirty or forty mysterious-looking forms squatting on the floor enveloped in gay coloured blankets. Their long, straight, black hair, parted in the centre, hung to below their waists and, falling over the high cheek-bones, nearly concealed their faces.

Through the dark greasy masses gleamed cold, uninquisitive, impassive, black eyes, and dabs of red and yellow ochre. Their *sang froid* was perfect. At our entrance they never moved, and scarcely seemed to see us. The interpreter spoke, and "Sitting Bull" replied, with a not over-polite grunt, "Ugh, Ugh." "Shake," said the interpreter to me. "Sitting Bull" put out his hand. I laid mine in it. And his closed with a grip, a slow, steady, unrelenting grip of steel. Presently a pain ran up my arm, I felt my bones would certainly crack. But with a desire to emulate the Indian calm, I stood it. And at last his grasp slowly relaxed. I was free. But I made up my mind that there should be no more shaking of hands with Indian chiefs for me.

We played two weeks at St. Louis (which was at that time the real starting point for California), where we were joined by Mrs. Knight Aston, just out from England, a tall, handsome, distinguished-looking woman. She brought her husband the most wonderful presents: a gold-mounted dressing-case, a diamond ring, diamond studs, &c., &c. I am sorry to say this magnificent lady turned out to be the notorious Mrs. Gordon Bailie, who, escaping (with much spoil) from London, left her faithful female servant to suffer three years' "hard" in her stead. "The presents" were part of the loot.

We arrived (a company of thirty-five, with a repertoire of ten operas) at San Francisco, May, 1877, put up at the Palace Hotel, and opened at the California Theatre, then under the management of John McCulloch. Our reception was most cordial and our success complete. The Press was with us all the time, the only adverse journalist being a particularly lively lady, the late lamented "Betsy B." I must say she went for me personally with a persistence worthy of a better cause, and asked "the Lord" continually what this earth had done that I should be placed upon it.

Everybody (especially the men everybodies) came to the theatre, and there was a beauty boom, like unto that of our first visit to New York, Miss Vesey, Miss Rose Stella, and Miss Cissy Durant, being especial pets, while Miss Florence Slater, who danced the Priestess in "Chilperic," nearly sent the boys crazy, as now and again, with vigorous kick, she sent her slipper up into the gallery. Strange to say, Mdlle. Sara, our prize kicker at 50*l.* per week, did not meet with universal approbation. The men liked Slater best, and the ladies professed themselves "real shocked." Whether it was her short ballet skirts (Slater wore long ones, to her toes) or—well, there is no knowing what it was. A theatrical audience is so difficult. In one city something will be hailed with acclamation by excited crowds, which in another is left severely alone, unseen—a horror.

Among the most prominent citizens of San Francisco, at that time, was Dr. Cornelius Hertz (of present "Panama" and Bournemouth fame), a member of the "Board of Health," one of the leading lights of society, the most fashionable physician and well-known "man about town" on the Pacific slope, intellectual, clever, and celebrated for his electrical cures. He treated Keene, the great "Wall Street" operator (once the friend, subsequently the victim of Jay Gould), and gave him so much electricity, also satisfaction, that Keene returned the compliment by giving Hertz 10,000 dols. He was profuse, extravagant, generous to a fault, and a regular godsend to the girls. Personally I liked him. He, in his official capacity and accompanied by some policeman very high up indeed in the city government, took us to Chinatown, where we saw everything—the opium dens, the tiny-toed *demi-monde*, the gambling, and the Fan Tan. We went into cellars, and cupboards, and down corridors, into which the nasty smells of

centuries had strayed and never got out any more;
to a Chinese restaurant, where gay young Chinese
"swells" were drinking tea and playing a game that
looked like "Thumbs up," "thumbs down"; to
the Chinese Theatre, where a great Chinese star had
just arrived. This was a striking entertainment,
but appealed more particularly to the olfactory
and auricular senses than to the artistic.

Dr. Hertz was the life and soul of everything,
and when we left he immortalized himself by pre-
senting one of the ladies with a beautiful plush
bag, lined with wash-leather. On the outside
was inscribed "Souvenir of the Golden State,"
inside was 1000 dols. in double eagles. This
was not the only coup made by the members of
the "Soldene" company. A bonarza king and
big racing man presented one of the ladies with
a 1250 dols. sealskin jacket, which jacket, to the
best of my belief, is in New South Wales to this
very day.

At this time, Mr. and Mrs. C. J. Williamson
(Miss Maggie Moore) were playing "Struck
Oil" in San Francisco. Maggie was the bright
particular idol. I went to see the piece, and
found her charming, *chic*, full of fun, but also
sympathetic.

I always thought Mrs. Williamson was Irish,

but she tells me she is Irish-American, born in 'Frisco—a 'Frisco girl who always wanted to be a 'Frisco boy—stage-bitten from when, as a tiny tot, she used "ter git inter" Jimmy's pants and go "wid Jimmy" into the "cullered pussun's Paradise"—the top gallery of the theatre. And when she first played parts, she wore "Jimmy's pants" till "Jimmy's pants" fitted "too snug," and she had to have a pair of her own. "And who's Jimmy?" says I. "My!—don't you know Jimmy?" says she. "Why, me brother, to be sure. I thought everybody knew Jimmy Moore."

While I was in the city, Mme. Modjeska came in from the Ranch, and made a most successful début, playing in English, with a pretty, fetching foreign accent. Madame was clever, also unfortunate, for within a short period of her first appearance she had her jewellery stolen. Of course the news was flashed from one end of the Union to the other. "Robbery of the Modjeska Diamonds— 100,000 dols." "Unreplaceable Heirlooms." "Heirlooms of the Polish Kings," and so forth. This, one of the most clever and successful advertisements at that time, has been worked to death since.

In San Francisco Mr. Chizzola engaged Mr. Edward Farley, an Australian, with a beautiful baritone voice and an excellent method; also two Californian girls—Miss Le Fevre and Miss Mattie Daniels, the latter a fine, handsome young lady of a rather quick temper, who carried in her work satchel, among her cottons and thimbles, and sometimes up her sleeve, a most formidable and handy weapon—an open razor, with the blade firmly bound to the handle by fine whipcord, a much patronised and effective weapon with the Chinese for performing the "Happy Despatch" on themselves or their favourite enemy.

In July we sailed for Australia on board the *Zealandia*. We steamed through the Southern Seas, but all too soon had a dreadful disappointment. The Hawaiian Government not having paid the postman, we did not call at Honolulu for the mail, and so missed what had been anticipated as a great treat—the "Hula Dancers," and lots of other things Lord Pembroke talks about in his book.

But soon we saw the Southern Cross, the flying fish, the nautilus, a white squall, lots of albatross, the sun drop suddenly into the sea, and the big moon rise, and the big stars shine over the big ship that moved along in stately splendour—moved along in seas of silver, and ripples of faint, rosy, phosphorescent flame.

In about a month, or thereabouts, we made Auckland, and the first white man that came aboard was Miles Paget. But white folks were at a discount with us just then. We wanted to see the Maoris, and we did not have to want long. There they were, waiting for us on the wharf. Fancy us comic opera cockneys finding ourselves really in New Zealand, face to face with a crowd of coffee-coloured, ox-eyed, tattooed natives! The ladies carried their babies on their backs, and their husbands' pipes in their ears, where other people carry their earrings. The Maori babies run the little vulgar boy at Margate very close indeed in the way of requiring a pocket-handkerchief, and the entire absence of anything resembling that necessary article.

Auckland was charming, with Mount Eden towering up into the sky, with tall Calla lilies growing in every crevice of the volcanic rocks, and watercresses (for nothing) waiting to be gathered in the city gutters. Auckland, where they called pheasants "spring chicken," where the hens roosted up in the trees, like blackbirds; where, on getting up in the morning, and taking a penny roll, a strong-bladed knife, and a walk along the shore, one got one's fill of fat fresh oysters; oysters that grew on the roots of trees; oysters that yawned in tiny shining sea pools; oysters that lived in the crevices and on the tops of rocks, over which the tide came splashing in white curly foam and feathers—you could take your choice, they were all there; Auckland, green and mossy and Scotch; so Scotch—shut your eyes and open your ears—you are in the "Cowcaddens."

Well, I fell in love with New Zealand—lovely New Zealand—with its opals, its fleecy flocks, its Kauri gum, its gold dust, its green stone, its filmy skies, its hills and dales, its locks and bays, its sands and caves.

On the day we landed there I went for a drive in a cab; the wheel came off, and out we got, when up came the local manager, Mr. de Lias, and persuaded Mr. Chizzola to break our journey to Sydney and play in Auckland. And we did, played for a month, to the capacity of the house. Then the August mail came along, and bidding "good-bye" to our New Zealand friends, we sailed for Australia.

My sister, like some of Mr. W. S. Gilbert's people, was always "very, very sick at sea," and the only thing that pulled her together was a game of cards. Clara was and is a born gambler, and with nothing in her hand will go 5l. better, and rake in the "pot," without turning a hair. Of course, coming up Sydney Harbour for the first time in one's life is an event. The scenery had to be (for future reference) looked at. Clara was on deck, packed up with pillows, playing " poker." " Do look," said I, " isn't it beautiful ? " But she was absorbed. Afterwards I said, " Why didn't you look at those lovely places ? " " How could I ? " said she, " I had a full hand." " Well," said I, " it's something disgusting, you missed all the fine points." " Oh, did I ? " said she, " Look here," and, lifting up her handkerchief, in her lap lay a little pile of shining sovereigns.

We landed in Sydney, the capital of sunny New South Wales, September, 1877.

CHAPTER XXIV.

Sydney in 1877—Sir Hercules Robinson (late Lord Rosmead) and Lady Robinson going to church—A nice-looking aide—Our hotel—The Oxford—My next-door neighbour, Miss Ada Ward—Julian Thomas, "The Vagabond"—Our four-in-hand—Botany Bay—Botany Bay heaths—Open at the Theatre Royal—"Geneviève de Brabant"—Theatre prices as contrasted with the States—The good memories of the Sydney folk—A House of Call for actors—My full-length portrait in soap—The beautiful harbour—The nostalgic ones in Australia—The station—Damper—Mutton and tea—Mr. "Ted" Lee—A little orphan—My farewell benefit—Presentation—Departure for Melbourne.

SYDNEY in 1877 was not like Sydney in 1892. I do not seem to remember much about the city. My retrospective impressions are bounded by George Street, King Street, the stage door of the Theatre Royal—and "Lady Macquaire's Chair." We put up at the Oxford Hotel, the proprietor then being Mr. Curran, who gave 5000*l*. to the Home Rule fund, and is now M.P. for Sligo. We had rooms opening on to a balcony, and looking straight over to St. James's Church, the oldest one in Sydney. I used to watch Sir

Hercules and Lady Robinson going to the morning service. Sir Hercules always stood on one side to let "me lady" pass; you see, the door was narrow, and her ladyship was not. There was a nice-looking aide too—a Captain St. John.

Next to the hotel, where the St. James's block now stands, was a pretty cottage, covered with green creepers, standing in a garden full of gorgeous flowers.

The next suite of rooms to ours at the hotel was occupied by Miss Ada Ward, the tragedian, and that well-known writer the "Vagabond" seemed to find a good deal of attraction there. He was a very frequent caller.

I remember King Street so well, because we had a four-in-hand, and every day went driving, and we always went down King Street and turned to the left up George Street; George Street seemed to lead everywhere.

We found the city very hot, and our first Sunday was passed at Botany Bay. We dined or lunched at the hotel, and lounged about the grounds in the afternoon. Botany Bay had never previously associated itself in my mind with anything floral—but with other things distinctly disagreeable. When I saw the ground covered with heaths of the most rare description; heaths, white, pink, yellow, purple, red, large waxy blooms, that in Covent Garden cost from 1s. to 2s. 6d. per spray, and big flowers as big as pint pots and quite as useful, and hedges of geraniums, and trees of fuchsias, then I began to understand that Botany Bay meant flowers— not convicts. That was a day to be remembered, for as we drove home the sun went down suddenly; there was, to our surprise, no twilight, no moon, all dark, four horses pretty fresh, a driver new to the country. We were nearly lost. But we got home to the hotel all right.

We opened at the Royal and a royal time we had. We began with "Geneviève de Brabant," but during our stay played the repertoire. I personally made a furore with "Silver threads among the Gold," "I love him so," and "Marriage Bells." The Theatre Royal was not too lovely, and the walls of the pit were greasy from much leaning against. Coming from an American theatre this was the more noticeable. The theatre was crowded every night, but the receipts seemed small after the States, where, in the class of house we played in, the lowest price was fifty cents. Coming to Australia, we found that people thought as much of a shilling as the Americans thought of a dollar.

Our ladies made the same old sensation. All the

boys lost their heads over them, and Miss Clara Vesey, Miss Stella, Miss Slater, Miss Durant, and Mdlle. Sara had great times. There were many husbands in the company, but they were kept in the background. We only played in Sydney six weeks, but the people were delighted with us, awfully good to us, and the impression we made was a lasting one. Why, in Sydney to this very day, people say, " Don't you remember, Madame Soldene, when you were at the old Royal? when you played ' so-and-so?' You used to do ' so-and-so,' and then you sang 'so-and-so.' I never forgot that song; I've got a copy of it now, somewhere."

Opposite the stage door of the theatre was a tavern, a regular theatrical house. In the windows, or rather on the windows, of that tavern, I could always see my portrait in every new part, nearly full-length, drawn with soap on the glass. I was very dignified in those days, and I am not quite sure I liked it. But it was life-like—the artist was decidedly clever. But it was not till I returned to Sydney in 1892 that I knew it was the work of the late Gus Wanganheim, a man I had heard spoken of as "such a good fellow," ready to help anybody or everybody to the extent of his ability.

In Sydney I played for the first time Barbe Bleu, and Miss Stella played Boulotte.

Lots of people came into town to see "Soldene." They "knew me in London." They had been to the "Phil" "hundreds of times." They had seen me play Drogan "every night." They had sent me bouquets "in the old days." Ah! those old days, "when they ran through all their money!" We were a long way from home, and these were emotional recollections. Fancy! no more money, no more bouquets. So many "stony broke" ones, too. It seemed terrible when people one knew said they had been "up country" in the "back blocks," in "the bush" for six months at a time, solitary, no letters from home, forgotten, never seeing anything but sheep, never eating anything but mutton and damper, never drinking anything but tea.

Well, I've had experience since, and I am afraid many of my reminiscent friends were, as the Americans say, "getting at me." I must have altered since then, for what sounded so dreadful at that time, "Life on a station," seems to me now most delightful.

We made lots of friends, and a most particularly nice one was Mr. "Ted" Lee. He told me many interesting things about the country, and how his father was one of the first men to get through the "Blue Mountains" to Bathurst, and what a wonderful sight it was when they first saw the plains. Like the rest of us, he was a wee bit sporty. I remember he went to Melbourne for "The Cup." I wired him to put me a fiver on his fancy. He did it, and I won 50*l*. Why can't I do it now?

We had lots of little outings, and I loved to go to "Coogee" Bay, to sit on the soft sands, to listen to the sighing of the soft winds, and to pick up shells, and pack them in little boxes to take home. No dirty, fussing, puffing, smoky trams in those days; no hotels, no houses, no Aquarium, no Embankments, no terraces, no improvements; nothing to be seen but the sheep-track, white on the farthest hill; nothing to be heard but the silver seas running up the silver sands. Then on Sundays we went to "Sandringham," or "Sans Souci," and had such good times. I made collections of shells, enough to fill two scuttles, or dust-bins. I suppose that's what they did do eventually.

Mr. Chizzola went one day on a kangaroo hunt with some Sydney gentlemen. When he came back he laid in my lap the prettiest, softest, dearest little grey darling, with bright shining eyes, a pretty black nose, tall ears, two short legs, like a rabbit, and two long ones, like—well, I don't know (I had never seen such legs before), and a very long tail; it was a wallaby, a baby wallaby. Such a tragedy! When he shot the mother at the hunt she had two little ones in her pocket, and so to keep the babies warm they laid the dead mother in the front of the fire, and there the "two orphans" slept all night.

The season finished up with my benefit. Patronized by the Governor and Lady Robinson, and the *entourage*, the suite and the *élite*, and all the city. It was really delightful, and Mr. Sam Lazaar, the local manager, made a speech, and presented me with a jewel casket made of an emu's egg and mounted in Australian silver. It was beautiful, and I appreciated it very much. We left Sydney with a good deal of regret and some apprehension, for people said, "What went in Sydney was a dead frost in Melbourne," and we had been so successful in New South Wales that we felt we should be an utter failure in Victoria.

CHAPTER XXV.

Overland to Melbourne on Cobb's coach—The driver—The nobbler—The cockatoos—The laughing jackass—Gundagai in 1877—The approach—Holes in the ground—A deserted gold-field—The patient Chinaman—What the goats live on—What we had for dinner—What I left behind—Open at the Opera House, Melbourne—"Geneviève de Brabant" —My landlady at St. Kilda—The Duke of Edinburgh's furs—A pretty house close to the sea—Mr. Creswick—An accident to Richard the Third—Why he married his Australian wife—"La Perichole" and the carpenter's dog— Old friends I meet—Dr. Neild, the eminent critic—A letter from Brandy Creek—Arrival of Mr. "Johnny" Caulfield—A visit to Mr. and Mrs. Saurin Lyster at Fern Tree Gully.

MOST of the company went to Melbourne by steamer, and got stuck in the mud outside that charming city, but four of us went overland. Such a journey, on a "Cobbs" coach, drawn by six young horses, who galloped up mountains and flew down them, driven by coachmen more or less under the influence of the weather. One told us he had been out on a "burst to a wedding, not slept for three nights," but should be all right when he had had a "nobbler." We looked forward with much pleasurable anticipation to the "nobbler," but were horrified when we saw it—"half a tumbler of whisky." Our driver tossed it off. He had not overstated its merits. It pulled him together splendidly, not that it made any difference in his driving, which was dare-devil and perfect, as was that of all the other boys. Fancy a track of soft sand, cut into deep ruts, piled up high in banks, winding in and out huge trees, sharp corners, unexpected fallen trunks, monster upturned roots, every kind of obstacle, six horses always galloping, the coach banging, creaking, swaying from side to side! then suddenly down we go, down over a mountain as steep as the side of a house, down into and through a rushing, roaring, tumbling, bumping, yellow river! Splash, dash. Then with a "Houp!" "Hi!" and a big lurch, out again and up the opposite side, galloping, always galloping, breathless; the driver shouting, cracking his whip, and the horses shaking the water from their sides, tossing their heads, and jingling their harness; then out on to the level, soft and springy, covered with mossy turf and beautiful trees like an English park; away over more sand, and leaving the mossy turf, and plunging through sharp, cutting, stiff, rusty-looking, tall grass, growing in huge tufts, far apart. At last we come to a hut, full gallop, and the driver, without any preparation, pulls the cattle up on their haunches, and you might cover them with a blanket, as the saying is. It was all lovely except for the jolting, and my hands were blistered with holding on. I liked to sit on the box, though it made one sick, not with fright exactly, but with excitement and the anticipation of some possible calamity.

My first flock of flying cockatoos disappointed me dreadfully. They looked exactly like a flock of pigeons. The driver told me that when one was wounded or hurt, and could not go on, the others despatched him, pecked his eyes out and tore him to pieces. I fancy I have seen something like that in more civilised regions. We went through groves, forests of gum trees, where there was no shade, but a delicious perfume. At night we heard the laughing jackasses, making an awful noise, but they laughed so well, that we joined in. That's another circumstance I've noticed in more civilised regions. At Gundagai there is an immensely long bridge, and we galloped over it in fine style. The approach to Gundagai, like every other mining town I have ever seen, was distinguished by a marvellous display of rubbish of all sorts, old boots, tin cans of every description (they do say the goats live on tin cans), meat cans, milk cans, oil cans, fish cans, fruit cans, old stays, old bonnets, old hats, old stockings, heaps of more cans, strewn for miles. It takes all the romance out of the scene. Gundagai was surrounded by large, middling, and small heaps of pale red sand; the place was full of "Holes in the ground," empty holes in the ground, as if herds of gigantic fox-terriers had been hunting out their best rabbits. This is the sign of deserted gold-diggings. Can anything be more lonely or more miserable? Nothing. I have seen them in gullies in America, in gullies and plains in Australia, in the heart of the mountains of California, in secret places of the Sierras, in little desert places in Nevada. But they are all alike—miserable, lonely, deserted, except by the wily, patient Chinaman, who goes over again the much gone over ground, making a Celestial's fortune out of the white devil's leavings, and disputing with the thin-legged, big-bellied, bearded goats, the abandoned tin cans. Still, at Gundagai there was a nice hotel. We had boiled fowls for dinner, and I left behind something I prized very much, a 5-cent palm leaf fan I had carried all the way from Cincinnati.

We opened at the Opera House, Melbourne, in "Geneviève de Brabant," and falsified our anticipations by making a big success. We lived at St. Kilda, at Mrs. Gardiner's. She was a furrier by trade, had a business in Melbourne, had prepared the furs for His Royal Highness the Duke of Edinburgh when he visited there (1868), and related the episode every day, sometimes twice a day. Some days it was very interesting, other days one found it monotonous; after many days it made one sick. She had a daughter named "Mary Jane." I remember it, because, when that young lady made any juvenile *faux pas*—and she was rather successful with that sort of thing—Mrs. Gardiner would observe (with a decided inflexion of the voice, signifying determination), "I'll warm you, Mary Jane Gardiner; I'll warm you."

The St. Kilda residence was a pleasant one—a long low house of one story, built on piles, with a broad passage running down the centre, and ten or twelve rooms opening off on each side. St. Kilda is close to and looking over the sea, so close to the sea, in fact, that a man-o'-war practising miles away had sent a big shot through the local pianoforte shop just before we arrived. It was a delightful place, but we seemed to have a good many hot winds there. They always gave me a horrible headache. In the same house lived Mr. Creswick, the Tragedian, who had just hit them very strongly in Melbourne, and was doing a great business. One night he came home in a terrible state. He had been playing "Richard the Third," and in the combat got cut on the head and had his teeth damaged. He was old, feverish, and fidgety. But we bathed his head, put him to bed, got his teeth mended, and he soon pulled round. During his stay in Australia he married the widow of a well-known Sydney professor. She, by the force of circumstances, had descended to keeping a lodging or boarding house. Mr. Creswick lived at her establishment in Sydney, and she first attracted his attention by bringing in his tea in silence, setting it down the same, and retiring ditto. Such a woman, to a studious man, was invaluable. He felt he must possess her for his very own, and they were married.

At Melbourne we added two operas to our repertoire—" La Perichole," with the expurgated last act, and "Girofle-Girofla." During the rehearsals of " La Perichole," when Mr. Campbell and I made our first entrance, the carpenter's dog, a fox-terrier, always accompanied us, and, wagging his tail, sat down with much gravity in the centre of the stage, with his back to the footlights, and, at one particular part of my opening song, lifted up his voice and gave a gruesome and most dismal howl. This went on for several mornings, the dog always howling at the same place, always paying the same tribute to my vocalisation. It was very funny and I thought we might utilise it. So for the performance we had a "Toby" frill made for my appreciator. We went on as the street singers, spread our carpet, tuned our mandolins, and commenced to sing. Directly I began doggy took up his cue beautifully, howling long and loudly. It was great—terrific applause and encore. Everybody said, "How clever! Who trained the dog?" Perhaps Mr. G. R. Sims, or *The Spectator*, or one learned in dog lore will explain why this dog at that particular part howled in misery and rage, and was a silent and sniffing and sympathetic angel during the rest of the performance.

Among the many old friends we met in Melbourne were Mr. and Mrs. Plumpton (Mme. Charlotte Tasca), and Mr. and Mrs. Bracy, and among the friends we made was Dr. Neild, who was excessively kind, and wrote most charming notices of our performances. He had a young son (not in the best of health), who took quite a fancy to me, and we used to go out driving together.

During my stay in Melbourne, one day I got a letter from a place called "Brandy Creek." It was from Mr. Weippert, once upon a time of Regent Street, London. It was very sad. He said he was there in that God-forsaken place in distress, and needed help to buy a piano to get his living. From his description "Brandy Creek" seemed to me to be about the last place in the world in which a professor of the pianoforte should set up his tent.

One night I had a most delightful surprise. "A gentleman would like to see me—a gentleman from England." It was "Johnny" Caulfield, one of the old Oxford chums, who since those days had married Miss Constance Loseby. But his health failing, he had come out in a sailing ship to Melbourne in search of a fresh fit out. I thought he was a ghost, but taking him home to supper we found he was not.

We had a good time in Melbourne. Mr. and Mrs. Saurin Lyster made us socially very welcome. We went out to their delightful place at "Fern Tree Gully," drove in a four-in-hand down a "corduroy" road constructed at an angle of 45°, had a lovely dinner and a lovely day, crept down the gully and saw the huge fern trees, rode bush ponies over stumps, through and over and under the trees, emulating and nearly sharing the fate of Absalom; saw heaps of cows milked mechanically, and the fine horses sent out to sleep in the paddock instead of in stables. Then in the evening we played halfpenny nap. I lost eleven shillings.

Of course; what can one expect, playing cards on a Sunday? We drove home to St. Kilda by the light of the moon, and very nearly had an awful spill. But a miss is as good as a mile, they say.

CHAPTER XXVI.

Miss Rose Stella and Miss Cissy Durant elope to Sydney—Miss Minna Fischer and Miss Maggie Liddell are engaged—A crossing to New Zealand—Killing an albatross—The chorus singer and his mother—Christmas Day at "The Bluff"—Dinner out of doors—What the imported girl thought of God and "The Bluff"—Christchurch—The weeping willows and black swans—The manager of the theatre—Sir Craycroft Wilson on the Indian Mutiny—Wellington, N.Z.—Where all the wind in the world goes to—A terrible return voyage to Australia—The psychological effect of the murdered albatross—The new Theatre Royal, Adelaide, opened March, 1878—An Australian magpie—What he did to the cat—What he did when he got to Putney—The chorus on horseback—A departure into the desert—At the gold mines—The Duke of Edinburgh's nugget—Where he got it—What he did with it—Visit to the exiles of St. Kilda—Farewell to Melbourne—Return to England August, 1878—What was going on when I arrived.

AT Christmas we left Melbourne for New Zealand, and just before we started Miss Rose Stella, yielding to the blandishments of Mr. Sam Lazaar, eloped (accompanied by Miss Cissy Durant) to Sydney, to appear in the forthcoming pantomime there. This troubled the management a good deal, but we pulled through, Mr. Chizzola engaging two local and well-known artistes, Miss Maggie Liddell and Miss Minna Fischer for some of the parts, Miss Clara Vesey and myself undertaking others. Miss Maggie Liddell was most entertaining, and told us many interesting stories of how on the west coast of New Zealand she had often gone through all sorts of difficulties to keep a concert engagement, riding alone through mountain passes, swimming her horse across foaming rivers, carrying her baby, placing herself full length along the horse's back and placing the baby along his crest to keep them both as dry as possible. We had a very good crossing, but on the way an albatross was caught and killed; this rather alarmed me, for I remembered the fate of the "Ancient mariner." The bird measured sixteen feet from tip to tip of his wings, and weighed goodness knows how much. He ultimately absorbed all the alum there was on the ship.

During the voyage there were some concerts in the saloon, and I, lying in my berth, heard a lovely tenor voice. "Who's that?" I asked, and was told it was one of the new chorus men engaged in Melbourne. He was quite young, and said his mother had instructed him he might join the company and take the salary, but must not *sing* in the choruses for fear of spoiling his voice.

We landed at "The Bluff" on Christmas Day, and I had a chop, a delicious mutton chop, and sat in the shining sun out on the grass to eat it. The young woman who waited on me was not exactly in love with her location, and expressed her opinion that "'The Bluff' was the end of the world and God had forgotten to finish it."

We opened at Dunedin (Dunedin is all Scotch) on Boxing Day to a great audience. "New Year's Eve" was a sensation, the streets impassable (nearly as bad as the "Salt Market," Glasgow), and we were taken home from the theatre by two or three policemen. Looking out of the hotel windows, one could have walked on the heads of the people, and the city was all alight with fireworks.

From Dunedin we went to Christchurch, a delightful place, full of weeping willows overhanging rippling streams, on which were floating beautiful, graceful, shining, *black* swans. The manager of the theatre was Mr. Hoskins, the ideal being I had such a passion for when a child, the Adonis of Sadler's Wells, whom in those prehistoric days I had longed to appropriate as an "Uncle."

At Christchurch we made great friends with Sir Craycroft Wilson, an old gentleman having a fine estate a little way out of town. He had been a magistrate in India during the Mutiny, and said he never got over the shock and the horrors of those times.

From Christchurch we went to Wellington. They say all the wind in the world goes to New Zealand, and all the wind in New Zealand goes to Wellington; and everybody knows a man from Wellington, because, no matter what part of the earth he is on, he always ducks and claps his hand to his hat when turning a corner.

We had a terrible voyage back to Australia, which I privately put down to the albatross business. There were storms, the hatches were battened down, and everybody was saying their prayers in the saloon, kneeling in a foot or two of water. I performed my devotions in my cabin (still pursued by the albatross). I made sure it was our last voyage. But, however, we made Melbourne, a bit battered, perhaps, but otherwise all right.

In March, 1878, we opened the new Theatre Royal, Adelaide, built and managed by Mr. J. Allison. I had to "speak a piece." I never was so nervous in my life. We sang "Girofle-Girofla." The theatre, a very fine one, was provided with every comfort, not only for the audience but for the artists—hot and cold baths, commodious dressing-rooms and other luxuries.

We found Adelaide dreadfully hot, but it was a beautiful city, the principal street a magnificently wide one, with an imposing Town Hall, and I think post-office. The houses were pretty, and it all struck one as being very clean.

At Adelaide I saw for the first time groves of olive trees. The grapes too were wonderful. I had a bunch weighing fourteen or fifteen pounds hung by a stout string in my dressing-room; every time I passed that bunch it grew smaller. Then there were tiny grapes, fairy ones, like the smallest of black currants. We went down copper mines and up mountains, especially the Eagle Mountain, driving up tremendous heights, at the edge and on the verge of hair-lifting precipices. When our buggy met another buggy we had to get out, and our buggy was hoisted on the side of the mountain to allow the other buggy to pass.

At the hotel on the summit we were introduced to an Australian magpie, with great gifts in the way of language. When we first saw him he was perched on the back of a sleepy black cat; occasionally the magpie woke the cat by pulling the longest hairs out of the inside of pussy's ears. We bought that magpie for 5*l.*, and when he got to

Putney he sang the national air of Australia, "Pop goes the Weasel," for all it was worth. The little boys of that riparian retreat clustered round my gates to listen to this wonderful bird from over the seas, and when I crossed Putney Railway Bridge, on my way to town, saluted me with "Pop goes the Weasel," so that I should not suffer under any misapprehension as to my identity being fully established. Poor, dear old magpie ; he died of consumption, and lies in a sunny corner of the sunny old-time Putney garden.

The company enjoyed themselves at Adelaide, went fishing and boating, had picnics, and driving and riding parties. We were continually meeting strings of mild " gee-gees," with the girls and boys of the chorus riding and having a good time. During my stay here, I saw a cavalcade depart from the city. It was like a picture out of the Bible. Hundreds of sheep and oxen, droves of horses, waggons, carts, and lots of men, an expedition into the interior, fitted out for three years. A pretty sight in Adelaide were the hundreds and hundreds of green love-birds flying about—" chatter," " chatter," " chatter."

We returned to Melbourne, visited Geelong (where, in the railway station, I saw a creaking, rusty old sign-board, with " Spiers and Pond " on

it), Bathurst, Ballarat, Sandhurst, and other places.
At Ballarat (which seems to lie in a basin) I went
with a Government mine inspector down mines,
into dead and gone river beds—muddy, soft,
sticky—and it seemed to me miles under the
earth; and looked down mines, dark, unused, insignificant in appearance, out of which had come
the treasures of the earth in prodigal profusion,
and listened to the crushing machines, the stamps
—such a dreadful, thumping, horrible, brain-
destroying noise—and did and saw everything
except "a piece of gold." And I told my inspector I was curious, and would like to see that;
he apologised, and, after a long search, found a
bit in the bottom of a crucible, about as big as a
coachman's button. The day before had been
"cleaning-up day," and all "the stuff" had been
sent away. I went to the mine where the Duke
of Edinburgh had picked a big nugget out of the
just ascended trolly of wet earth. Of course, the
managers and great guns begged His Royal
Highness's acceptance of his find, and His Royal
Highness graciously put it in his pocket. They
told me the load had been "salted" for the
occasion. I noticed they did not salt one for
me.

On my return to Melbourne in June, I went to

say "Good-bye" to the "exiles of St. Kilda," expatriated by the "family" for marrying in haste, only, I am afraid, to repent at leisure. They were the Honourable Mr. and Mrs. Wyndham Stanhope, Miss Camille Dubois, of the Lyceum "Little Faust" days. The pair were rather impecunious, and not provided with passage money, but lived in a pretty little flower-decked house, also in hopes of being "cabled" home; and, as a matter of fact, I think they returned to England very soon after we did.

My farewell engagement and benefit at Melbourne was a gratifying success, and I cannot do better than introduce a Press notice of my last appearance, a notice cut from *The Illustrated Sporting and Dramatic News*, of London, dated December 21st, 1878.

"Before leaving for Europe, Miss Soldene was tendered a 'farewell benefit,' which took place at the Theatre Royal, Melbourne, under the patronage of the Governor and Lady Power, and the mayor and corporation of the City of Melbourne, and was presented with a testimonial by Mr. Coppin in the following terms: 'Madame Soldene,—I have been requested by a few of your friends to present you with a small token of their esteem and admiration upon the occasion of your farewell benefit and departure from the colonies. Although this cup and salver are intrinsically of little value, I trust that they will serve to remind you of the high estimation in which you are held as an accomplished artist, whilst they revive some agreeable recollections of your visit to the Australian colonies. I have also the gratification to inform you that you have been elected a life governor of the Dramatic and Musical Association of Australasia, and that an illuminated tablet has been voted by the council, with the following inscription:—"Testimonial presented to Miss Emily Soldene in acknowledgment of valuable services rendered for the benefit of the Dramatic and Musical Association of Australasia at the Theatre Royal, Melbourne, on Saturday afternoon, May 26th, 1878." I can assure you that you will take with you the sincere gratitude of the entire profession, and our best wishes for your health, happiness, and future prosperity.' Miss Soldene sailed for home the next morning in the steamship *Chimborazo*, which, under the command of Captain Herbert Brown, made the quickest passage on record, the distance being accomplished in thirty-seven days twenty-one hours."

I don't mind mentioning in strict confidence that from that day to this, September 15th, 1896,

I have never set eyes on the "Illuminated Tablet."

When I arrived from Australia, August 12th, 1878, Mrs. Langtry was the reigning beauty; Sheil Barry was a sensation at the Charing Cross Theatre, as Gaspard the Miser, in "Les Cloches de Corneville;" the Alhambra was playing to empty benches, and "H.M.S. *Pinafore*" at the Opera Comique to half salaries.

CHAPTER XXVII.

Reappearance in London, September 16th, 1878—At the Alhambra—"Geneviève de Brabant"—How many persons paid at the doors that night—The cast—M. Jacobi as a conductor—The mise-en-scene—The premières of the ballet—Maharajah Dhuleep Singh—His diamonds—His caviare—The Alhambra directors—The Alhambra manager—Sir Augustus Harris in 1878—Sir Gordon Cumming—The "Crutch and Toothpick Ball"—Purchase of "Carmen"—Production, Theatre Royal, Leicester, May, 1879—Miss Florence St. John—"Carmen" in Liverpool, Prince of Wales's Theatre—"Carmen" in Dublin Gaiety Theatre—What the car-drivers said—What the flute-player wrote in the flute part—"Carmen" in Glasgow—A lunch with Admiral Popoff—What we all came away with.

ON Monday, September 16th, 1878, I made my reappearance in London at the Alhambra Theatre, then under the management of Mr. Charles Morton, playing Drogan in "Geneviève de Brabant." That night 4000 persons paid at the doors. In the cast were Miss Constance Loseby as the Duchess; Messrs. Marshall and Bury, the two Gendarmes; Miss Clara Vesey, the Pet Page; Mr. AyneslyCook, the Duke; Mr. J.B. Rae, the Burgomaster; Miss Rose Lee, Brigette; Mr. Lewens,

Golo; Mr. Dallas, the Hermit; Mr. Kelleher, Charles Martel. Among the maids of honour were the Misses Bertie, Stuart, Barber, Norton Rivers, Devine, Vito, and others.

M. Jacobi was the conductor—for me, an ideal one. Of course, everybody can see how he conducts for the ballet. But to fully appreciate him you must be a vocalist. It does not matter whether you are full of sentiment, or full of devilment (a singer is a capricious creature, and not always under control), in good form or bad form, ill or well, he is always with you, waiting, coaxing, supporting, giving way to little unexpected fads of expression, phrasing, or breathing. Attentive to every movement, to every sigh, he anticipated what you were going to do, and *let* you do it. The result was a delightful unanimity, and perfect success.

The return of "Geneviève" was a triumph, the business abnormal, the notices good and congratulatory. As for me, personally, they thought I was a little better than when I went away.

The opera was mounted splendidly, the dresses being superb. There was a row of maids of honour, who looked like mediæval duchesses, stiff and magnificent, in brocade, embroidery and fur. I need scarcely say the pages were extremely well looked after, and got as little clothes as possible. All the principals were radiant. There was only one old costume on the stage, that was mine. Call it superstition, perhaps it was; but nothing would induce me to put on a new dress. Re-trimmed and spangled, I glittered beautifully, and passed among the crowd. In the second act was danced a " Bohemian ballet," in which Mdlle. Rosa distinguished herself. At this time Mme. Pertoldi was the première danseuse, and Mdlle. Gillert the première mime. Our most constant visitor behind the scenes was the Maharajah Dhuleep Singh, very amiable and nice. He wore some wonderful diamond rings, and would often insist upon my wearing them for the stage. I was always glad to get off, and return them. One Sunday he gave a swell dinner at Vevey's, and, in introducing to my notice some very fine caviare, said he always sent his own man to Russia, who brought it right through—no intermediate parties. In the Alhambra chorus was one very tall, elegant girl. She filled the ideal bill, got twenty-five shillings a week, wore sealskin, sable, and magnificent diamonds, came in her carriage and pair, and her footman waited at the stage-door with her cloak. She could go into the directors' room at any time without knocking at the door, and sometimes gave His Highness the Maharajah a lift. Her portrait as "Mrs. Marini" figured in all the photographers' windows, and, taken altogether, she was a very fashionable person indeed. The girls used to coax her and say, " Hi say, Mareenee, send hus hup er bottle er fizz ; won't yer, Mareenee ? " And "Mareenee," who was charming and splendid and good-natured, did it.

Among the directors of the Alhambra was Mr. Winder, a nice gentlemanly man, a good manager, and connected with music halls, notably the Metropolitan, for a number of years ; Mr. Leader, always associated in my mind with the box office of the Italian Opera, Her Majesty's Theatre (under the colonnade), who, when in the Greenroom, invariably forgot he was *not* in the smoking room ; Mr. Nagle, the champion bill poster ; Mr. Sutton was the chairman, bumptious and important. Mr. Morton, deferential and self-effacing, got along very nicely with these gentlemen. Sometimes after the performance, going through the directors' box to get out the front way quickly, we met a young slim gentleman (good-looking too) just coming in, with whom we would have a parting B. and S. Sometimes the young gentleman walked across with us to our lodgings in Charles Street, Haymarket, and shared our modest little supper. The young slim gentleman was Mr. Augustus Harris, of the Criterion Theatre.

During the season, a committee of gentlemen (prominent among whom was Sir Gordon Cumming) connected with a prevailing and fashionable fad, just then in its first days, wishing to give a very select and exclusive ball, approached me with the request that I would make out a list and invite those ladies of the professional world I preferred. I did so. And "The Crutch and Toothpick Ball," at Willis's Rooms, was remarkable for the beauty and *chic* of the women, and the undeniable and exceedingly good form of the men.

Early in 1879, having secured from Messrs. Chondens of Paris the provincial rights of "Carmen," I, in May, produced it at the old Theatre Royal, Leicester. The interest taken by the town was immense, and the patient audience stood in the streets for hours before the doors opened.

One day, while at Parravicini's office in Duke Street, engaging the company for this tour, I saw a young lady who, I had been told, was a good artiste and a fine musician. The young lady was decidedly pretty, charming in manner, but fragile in appearance. I did not engage her, considering that she had not sufficient physique to sing every evening in a heavy repertoire. In acting on this opinion, I missed a good artiste, but she found her opportunity a little later on, which she would not have done had she been travelling with me. " Mme. Favart " was being rehearsed at the Strand. Miss Fanny Josephs was to play the part, but that fell through; she gave it up; my young lady was sent for. She sang, and caught the town. The young lady was Miss Florence St. John.

It was generally conceded that my " Carmen " was a good one. I had a natural turn for the tragic, and my acquired taste and experience in comic opera enabled me to give many little touches which had not been thought of before. It was a very difficult opera to produce; and there was no end of bother with the orchestra. Fancy, three trombones all wanting 6*l*. per week each! The work was extremely exhausting for the principal singers. But at the Prince of Wales's Theatre, Liverpool, Mr. Lely and I made a record, which is still unbroken, singing " Carmen " every night for three consecutive weeks to crammed houses.

In Dublin, when the bills and announcements came out, there was great excitement among the car-drivers. They said, " See that now, see what Soldene is bringing us, an opera of our own, the opera of ' The Carmen.' " We had matinées at the Gaiety, Dublin; rather an innovation in those days; and in the book of the flute-player is the following lyric, written in pencil :—

> "Soldene's collaring all the chips,
> Bizet's gone to heaven,
> And I sit here a playing the flute
> For a paltry three-and-eleven." [1]

In the autumn of 1879 we went to Glasgow, playing "Carmen," of course. But the principal event of this visit was being invited by Admiral l'opoff, the chief constructor to the Russian Navy (and who, since that time, has constructed a circular ship, which in the Baltic went round and round and never stopped) to lunch with him on board the Tsar's new and magnificent yacht, the *Livadia*, then being built at Messrs. Elders' yard at Gourock. Of course an invitation from such a personage was a great honour, and we "toiletted" accordingly. Fancy our disgust when, on getting out of the train, we were met by a dirty, dusty, snuffy old man, buttoned up to his chin in a military, but fearfully wine-stained, coat, with dabs of grease all down the front—it was the Admiral. But our disgust was intensified when he led the way, not to an Imperial carriage, as we had fondly pictured, but

[1] Morning performance, half salary.

to the tram; such a dirty tram, too. Still, when we got to the yard we found the yacht was magnificent, so were the officers, so was the lunch, which was lavish and extravagant to a degree. So was the Admiral, when we got used to him; and we all came away with a little present.

CHAPTER XXVIII.

On the Plains—A ride on the train—The oasis—Archibald Forbes—Anecdote of Forbes, D'Oyley Carte, and P. T. Barnum—Barnum appears for my benefit—Salt Lake City in 1881—People I meet—The cornet-player of the Crystal Palace Orchestra—An "extra girl" frae Glaskie—How the Salt Lake girls wore their tights—How many wives each Mormon brought to the show—How the ladies of the opera company went to their hotel—The legend written on the rocks and boulders of Salt Lake—The City of Eureka—Its theatre—Its men, manners, ways and means—The chorus girl that played the piano in the gambling saloon and what she got for it—Why she did it—Who she was—" Colorado Springs "—" Pike's Peak "—" The Garden of the Gods "—B. and S.—" Leadville "—The gambling saloon—The shooting—" Fork's Creek "—The suicide of Henry Hersee, junr.—Where and when they found the remains.

In the autumn of 1880 once more to America, and in 1881, crossing the Plains on my way to 'Frisco, I heard that the engine and driver on our train were the same with whom the Duke of Manchester had done a long ride when going West. Instantly I wished to follow the illustrious example of his Grace. Into the cab I clambered and rode for thirty miles; but never again!

There was such swaying to and fro, not to say pitching and rolling, and such vibration that every revolution of the wheels seemed to pass through my body. At last, when I was quite black and blue, we stopped at a little place called Humboldt—an oasis in the desert, not only a disagreeable, sandy, sage-bush desert, but a saline, pickling, prickly desert, that covered one's lips with sharp acrid salt, and filled one's eyes with sharp acrid tears. Humboldt was green, and soft, and pleasant to look upon, with waving shade trees, and a fountain in which were gold-fish who jumped and seemed to sparkle and crackle in the sun. We had nice tea and coffee, and custard pies, *mirabile dictu*, "without any flies." The east-bound train was there at the same time, and on the platform stood a gentleman wearing tweeds and a Norfolk jacket. About him there was that unmistakable something that marks the Englishman all over the world. "I wonder who that is," said I to somebody; "I seem to know his face." "Of course, everybody knows his face," replied somebody; "it's Archibald Forbes, the great war correspondent." It has always been a matter of regret to me that I did not go up to him and have a talk; I certainly should if I were to meet him now.

Michael Gunn told me a funny story of Archibald Forbes and D'Oyly Carte being in New York, and P. T. Barnum inviting them to visit him at Bridgeport, Conn. The celebrated showman was a total abstainer, and more picturesque than particular in his expressions. " You boys can cum an' stay—I guess yer can cum stay fer a month ; but mind, no ' bug juice.' "

Barnum had a daughter married and settled in Southport, Lancashire, and the old man came over every year and had a good time with her. I was playing at the Winter Gardens during one of these visits, and when my name went up for the usual Friday night benefit, he " guessed he'd come and speak a piece." Of course, I was more than delighted, and big bills announced the fact that the world-renowned showman, Mr. P. T. Barnum, would address the audience on the auspicious occasion. There was a tremendous house, and in the middle of the evening he went on, and had a grand reception. But having got on, he would not come off, and there he stood and talked for one hour and fifteen minutes.

In April, 1881, coming east from San Francisco, I visited for the first time Salt Lake City, a beautiful place, full of fruits and flowers. On each side of the streets are tall shade trees, and a tiny running streamlet tinkling all the time. In the distance are the mountains covered with snow; there are fine hotels, fine houses, fine stores. "Latest Paris fashions for the opera season" struck me as being remarkably appropriate. I went to see the "Tabernacle." At the door a man lifted his hat. "How do you do, madame? You don't recollect me? I was the cornet in the orchestra when you played at the Crystal Palace last year."

The theatre was large, shaded with lime trees, smelling deliciously. When I went on the stage, the stage manager was looking over the most likely candidates for the important rôle of " extra girls." Among them was one with remarkable hair, red, and most abundant. I recognised her at once. She had been with me at the Gaiety Theatre, Glasgow, the Christmas of 1879. "Why, Maggie," said I, " How in the world did you get here?" "Well," said she, "I come with mother and father, an' father's got a new wife." "A new wife! and what's your mother say to that?" "Ah, weel, she's a' richt; she had ter 'seal' her to father. It's th' law." "And how old are they?" "Father's seventy-two, mither's sixty-eight, an' th' new wife's tew years younger than me. I'm ter be 'sealed' masel' soon."

That night, about a quarter of an hour before

the curtain was to go up, Mrs. Quinton, my wardrobe mistress, said, "Can I bring in some of the local girls for you to see?" "Yes," said I, "What's the matter?" She brought them in. These daughters of the desert had got into tights with all their petticoats on, and when they turned round presented a most extensive and wonderful sight. The house was filled to its capacity, almost entirely with women, who had evidently paid a visit to the "Paris latest fashions," and there were nodding feathers and flowers all over the place. I learned that, this being the first night, the audience was most wealthy, aristocratic, and select, and each man had brought from ten to twelve wives. The members of our company had great fun, the gentlemen taking the ladies home in Mormon fashion. Mr. Marshall, the stage manager and doyen of the crowd, marched at the head. All the girls followed in Indian file, some gentlemen brought up the rear, and the ladies were seen safely into their respective hotels.

On returning to Ogden, *en route* for Denver, we were much cheered by seeing painted on the rocks and boulders that historic and heart-stirring legend, "Woa, Emma." During this tour we visited "Eureka," a mining town, the only one I

ever saw in the States without a church. The
theatre was built of weather-boards, sawdusted,
and lit with petroleum lamps. The lime-light was
the head-light of an engine, lent by the railway
company and placed in the wings. The dressing-
rooms were calico screens. The lowest admission
was five dollars, and the air was so full of sulphur
you had to walk about with a pocket handkerchief
to your mouth. Eureka was a dreadful desert of
dry, sandy mountains; on each side of the narrow
road were gambling saloons, and down it ran little
streams bordered with green. The little streams
came from the reducing works, and the green was
a mineral deposit from the same source. One of
the gambling saloons captured a chorus girl of ours.
She could play the piano well; she got eight
dollars per day, and a percentage on the drinks.

We left Eureka at 4 a.m., and, as we walked
past the saloon, heard through the thick and
poison-laden air the tinkle of the piano played
by Alice C——. I saw her afterwards in San
Francisco in 1891. She brought me as a present,
a lovely canary in a lovely cage, and was in great
form; had married the proprietor of the Eureka
Saloon, with whom she was now keeping one in
'Frisco. "Oh, Alice," said I, "I *was* so sorry when
you stopped in that dreadful place." " Well, you

see, madame," said she apologetically, "I had my child to keep." Alice was the widow of poor Tom Melling, the Oxford harmonium player, who was drowned in the river at York, leaving a young wife and baby.

We went to Colorado Springs, the country of health, where every consumptive patient is cured, where you sleep under tents high up in the mountains, where the air is so dry that your bucket of water evaporates in the night, where soda-water, bright and sparkling, springs from the earth, and nothing is wanted to complete your happiness but a little Hennessy to go with it; where every morning we looked up to "Pike's Peak," and every afternoon drove out to Manitou—"The Garden of the Gods."

We played at Denver, then went on to Leadville; Leadville—10,000 feet above the level of the sea, where there are no horses, no cats, no dogs, and you have to walk slow; Leadville—the Silver City of the West, where the walls of my dressing-room glittered with the precious stuff, and the roads were paved with it; where cabbages cost half a dollar, and radishes are five cents each. At Leadville we saw some shooting. It was 5 a.m.; we were walking to the depôt, passing through the principal street, lined on each side with gambling saloons. The dawn was just breaking, when out from one of the houses tumbled a little crowd—Bang-bang-bang. Two were left in the road, the others went back to their game.

Then, on our way to "Golden" City, at a place called "Fork's Creek"—the junction of North and South Clear Creek, and twenty-eight miles west of Denver—we had to wait for a train, and young Henry Hersee threw himself from the trestle bridge of the railroad into the rocky chasm below, filled with a rushing mountain torrent, storming from a recent waterspout, running twenty miles an hour. I can see his blue eyes now, looking straight out of the water up to the sky. Then his head went "bash" on a big rock, and we saw him no more. Six weeks afterwards his remains were found at a place called "Beaver Brook," twenty-two miles west of Denver; his body was ground by the rocks to a pulp, and his clothes had disappeared.

CHAPTER XXIX.

My adventure with a St. Louis Sheriff—How he arrived twenty minutes late.

DURING this 1880-81 tour, I had many interviews with many sheriffs, and was being continually "arrested" or "attached." My managers, Messrs. Jarvis and Froom, made contracts for me to appear at certain places, then made other contracts for me to appear on the same night at certain other places 500 miles away. My name being at the head of the bill, I was held responsible. The consequence was that we were always arriving at places where the sheriff turned up about 8.30 p.m., and sequestered the receipts at the suit of Messrs. So-and-so, for breach of contract. When they had got all the cash they could, they would attach the wardrobe, which was my private property, lent to my managers at a certain sum per week, which I never got. This was all very worrying, and under the advice of a lawyer at St. Louis, I, for valuable consideration, made over the whole of my wardrobe, both personal and professional, to my wardrobe master, Mr. Quinton, who, with his wife, had been with me many years and could be trusted. And one day the sheriff came off second best. A deed was drawn up and executed at St. Louis, but to make the deed valid it must be filed at the City Hall. No sooner had the paper been signed and carried off by Quinton, than a sheriff (a most polite person), waited on me at my hotel, The Planters' House, and "regretted" he had a claim against me for 2000 dols., "breach of contract," &c.; that he proposed attaching my baggage and me personally; that I must consider myself under arrest, and I must on no account leave my rooms.

I asked him had he been to the theatre. He said, "No," he was on his way there, and should attach the wardrobe, till the claim was settled. "Well," I said, "I thought it would be better if he would stay with me, while I sent a messenger for the manager to come right along." He didn't mind. So I rang the bell for some whisky and cigars, and asked the sheriff would he pass me the writing materials. He did so. I wrote a note to Quinton to rush off to the Town Hall and file the deed at once, fastened it up, rang the bell. The bell-boy came, I passed the note over the table to my friend. He was too much of a gentleman to look at the direction and passed it to the boy. My arrest was not very painful. My arrester sat and talked, drank his whisky, and smoked his cigars. Quinton made no reply to my note. Time was getting on, and I was getting in agony. Conversation flagged a bit, and I brought out some albums of celebrities. Two hours passed, and my visitor " guessed " as the manager didn't come he must be off to the theatre. At last I could not keep him any longer. He went, but before going put me on my parole not to leave the hotel. I broke it and rushed off to the Barnum House where Quinton lived. Mrs. Quinton was in a dreadful state. " Oh, madame, we've been out; William only just got your note and has gone to the City Hall now." I fled back to the Planters' House, and threw off my things. Close behind me arrived Quinton, breathless. "Just in time, madame," panted he, "I filed the deed five minutes before the office closed."

My friend the sheriff arrived at the theatre twenty minutes too late. The deed had been registered quite fifteen minutes.

CHAPTER XXX.

At Chester—The detectives—The Irish troubles—A letter from Mr. Gladstone—The old Theatre Royal, Southampton—An old artist's memories of it in 1846—The manager in those days—Miss Fanny Vining (Mrs. John Wood)—Her conquests—Her marriage—The sisters Cushman—The company—Where the walking gentleman was in 1878.

In May, 1883, I visited Chester with "Carmen." Mr. Gladstone was staying at the Rectory, Hawarden, and I drove out to ask him to give his personal patronage on the following Friday night. It seemed a strange thing to me that as I drove through the country lanes I noticed so many people about; every fifty or a hundred yards there was a man sauntering along, coming or going from Hawarden way, and they all looked hard at me and the carriage and the driver. Every now and then a face would appear above the hedge, another would be regarding with much interest the bursting blooms of the already blossoming May; another with vacant eye stood stock still while we passed him. Somehow these people aroused and irritated my theatrical instincts—they were out of the picture—they did not agree with the situation, and they had no local colour, and were out of tone with their environment. When about half a mile from the Rectory, a man stopped the carriage (an open one), and, glancing at me, said something in a low tone to the driver, who, replying, nodded his head and went on, but rather slowly. "What did that man want?" said I, leaning forward. "He wanted to know your name, mam." What impudence, thought I. When we got within sight of the Rectory, another man stopped us, and said we could not go any further. "Why?" said I. "Orders, mam," said he. "But," said I, "I want to see Mr. Gladstone." "Sorry, mam; not possible." "Why?" "Can't tell you, mam." "Well, can I send a note?" "Yes, mam." I had one prepared and the man took it. Then he came back. "I gave it to the butler, mam; he will bring an answer." Presently a middle-aged man, wearing indoor livery, came to the gate. The man on duty went to him, and returned with the message: "Mr. Gladstone's compliments to Miss Soldene, and he will write." "I'm so sorry, Miss Soldene," said our detainer, "I could not let you pass, but our orders are strict—nobody can pass.".

"But why?" "Well, you must ask someone else that." This was in the time of the Irish troubles, and Mr. Gladstone was strongly guarded by detectives. These were the men I had seen sauntering and interested in the general agricultural progress of the land around Hawarden. Mr. Gladstone did not visit the theatre, but that evening I got a letter from him, not written by a secretary, but by himself. The letter was as follows :—

"Hawarden Castle,
"Chester.

"Mr. Gladstone presents his compliments to Madame Soldene, and is sincerely sorry, as is Mrs. Gladstone, that they are not able to come into Chester for the purpose of attending at the Royalty Theatre. They wish well to Madame Soldene's enterprise, and she is at liberty to make use of their name this week, if she thinks fit.

"May 17th, 1883."

A little later in the year, or it may have been perhaps in 1884, I played a week at Southampton, at the old Theatre Royal, and found that for Mr. Edward Marshall, my stage manager and principal comedian, the place was full of memories. "Ah," said he, looking round the dingy little Green-room, "it was just there," pointing to an old settle, "I first saw Mrs. John Wood." "How delightful," said I, "tell me all about it." "Well," he went on, "in—in—yes—in 1846, the theatre was under the management of Mr. W. Parker, a local professor of dancing, and not at all a bad actor. I was engaged for second low comedy, and to sing and dance between the pieces. Soon after I joined, there arrived a Miss Fanny Vining and her sister, daughters of Mr. and Mrs. Henry Vining, who I think at that time were members of Mr. Osbaldiston's company, at the Royal Victoria Theatre, New Cut, Lambeth. Miss Fanny," said Mr. Marshall with a sigh, "made a great sensation. She was a perfect little beauty—deep, dreamy eyes, curled lashes, peachy cheeks, and a dewy rosebud for a mouth. She played the mischief in the theatre. All the boys were in love with and laid siege to this charming fortress. But John Wood, principal comedian, was the lucky dog. And at the end of the season they were married. I think," said he hesitatingly, "but am not quite sure, I think they ran away." "I believe you were in love with her yourself," said I. "Well, Madame," said he, "upon my word there are more unlikely things than that." Then he went on: "The sisters Cushman were here in my time, singing duets. Charlotte had a very fine voice, and much musical taste. Mrs. Nisbet and Miss Patty Oliver were members of the company; Tom King played the lead, and Tom Bellairs was our walking gentleman. Do you know, when we were in Australia in 1878—after all those years—I saw Bellairs. He was the proprietor of the principal hotel, a sort of Tattersall's, attached to the racecourse at Melbourne, and mayor of a suburban township."

CHAPTER XXXI.

"Frivoli" at Drury Lane, 1886—The company—A sensation—
The two Cæsars—Mr. Augustin Daly and Mr. Augustus
Harris—Lord Alfred Paget—A dried haddock and a bottle of
brown sherry—Tea with the girls—Lord Alfred's sartorial
eccentricities—Lord Alfred as a city man—Lord Alfred
introduces the bangle cult in the ballet—The last time I
saw him—" Good-bye"—What the ballet said when his will
was published—A card from "Jack the Ripper"—A
midnight walk in London—The white arrow—Lord
Mandeville—Bessie Bellwood—" Wot Cheer, 'Ria?"

In March, 1886, Mr. Augustus Harris engaged me to play in M. Hervé's opera "Frivoli," to be produced at Drury Lane. In the cast were Mme. Rose Hersee, Miss Marie Tempest, Mr. Harry Nichols, and Miss Kate Munroe, beautiful, pleasant, perfectly-dressed Kitty. Mr. Harris (assisted by Mr. Charles Harris) conducted the rehearsals.

One morning there was a sensation. So many people being engaged in the spectacle, Mr. Harris had a chair placed in the centre of the stage, standing on which he could more effectively arrange the disposition of his forces. During the rehearsal a card was brought in. Of course, the moment his attention was turned everybody's tongue went loose, a regular "chatter," "chatter," like a big school. "Silence, ladies and gentlemen," said the chief sharply; then mounting the chair and addressing the man who had brought the card, said: "What was the message?" "Mr. Augustin Daly's compliments, sir, and he and his friends would like to look over the theatre." Mr. Harris stretched out his arm, and pointing over the heads of the people to the swing door through which one came from the stage entrance on to the stage, and at which door a little group of gentlemen could be seen, said in a very distinct and determined tone: "Show Mr. Augustin Daly and his friends out."

I afterwards heard that one of Mr. Harris's companies had been playing at the Theatre Royal, Brighton, and Mr. Augustin Daly on the Saturday gave a matinée there. A number of Mr. Augustus Harris's people went into the pit before the doors were opened, and Mr. Daly had them removed, and there you have the *casus belli*.

One day after a long, fatiguing rehearsal, going out at the stage door, I met Lord Alfred Paget coming in. He was carrying a rather large rush basket, a fishmonger's basket. "What have you got there?" said I. "Well," said he, "it's haddocks, dried haddocks, and a bottle of brown sherry. I am going to have tea with some of the girls. Will you come?"

Lord Alfred was peculiar, but pleasant, agreeable, and more than interested in the theatre and theatre folk, by whom he was much respected. Some people thought him rather awful, and Mrs. Nye Chart would not allow him behind the scenes at her theatre. But for my own part I must say I found him anything but terrible. He was always busy, and invariably shabby, wearing a frock coat that had seen no end of better days, and round his neck a large silk and rather greasy handkerchief (generally a "birds-eye") tied like an old-fashioned stock. His hat was picturesque—old and dreadful—with the nap always the wrong way, and in a state of violent remonstrance. He was director of any number of companies, and as a rule he carried a bag, a carpet bag, and rather a large one, too. He often popped into the theatre at rehearsal, but only for a moment, being "Eastward-bound," so he would say, "going to the city" in fact, to which he travelled on top of the "'bus." After one of my American journeys (not having seen him for a year or two) I met him in the Strand. He was still carrying the bag, and came to the point at once. "Dear Emily," said he, "dear old friend; *where* can I buy some long black silk gloves? There's a girl can't go on to-night till I get them for her."

Lord Alfred introduced the bangle cult among the ballet. When he returned from India, where he accompanied the Prince in 1875, he brought home a sack full of bangles, none of them too expensive, and the dancing girls and the chorus went "tinkle, tinkle, tinkling," about the theatre and shaking little tiny silver bells, till it got on one's nerves. Every girl had a dozen bangles on her wrists, and it was only by the practical remonstrances of the stage manager, who murmured something about "fines," that they were kept off their ankles.

The last time I met Lord Alfred was at the Waterloo Station, a few months before his death. I was waiting for my train to Barnes. He was, he told me, waiting for some members of his family who were coming from—I forget where. Anyway, the train arrived, but no family. He was vexed: "One hour and a half," said he, "have I been here; waited two trains. Now I shall go. Good-bye." "Good-bye," said I.

It was the final good-bye. I never saw him again. Everybody was very surprised when they heard he had left £100,000. "Fancy!" said the ballet, rattling their bangles, "with that coat too."

During the run of "Frivoli," we got a great fright. Mr. Harris received through the post a card, a threatening card, from "Jack the Ripper," and that deadly persuasive person not only expressed himself in very definite and distinct terms, but endorsed his views by impressing upon the document a bloody thumb and finger. Mr. Harris was kind enough to show us the card, and how we crowded round and gloated over the horrid thing, and the fascination of the bloody sign was irresistible.

Talking about "Jack the Ripper," one night, it must have been in 1888, I had been to Drury Lane on some business, and left there late, after twelve o'clock. The rush from the theatres was over, the public-houses were closed, the streets were quiet and empty. There was a moon, with dark scudding clouds, but altogether pretty clear, so I concluded to walk to Charlotte Street, Bedford Square, where I was then living. In the next house to me Lord Mandeville had rooms, and, strange to say, so had the Lady Elizabeth Bellwood. I walked down Russell Street, from the stage door of Drury Lane, and as I turned into Bow Street saw drawn on the pavement in chalk, an arrow, a broad white arrow, pointing north. I had not gone a hundred yards before there was another, and at Merryweather's corner was still another, pointing slightly to the left. I crossed over to the west side of Endell Street, and had not gone far before I saw another, still pointing straight ahead. By this time I felt creepy and seemed to understand the arrows were a direction, also that I must follow that direction. I walked to the end of Endell Street, and then could see no more, they were finished. I was glad I had distanced them. It was nothing, only my fancy, but crossing the road to Bellew's Chapel I came on the direction again, broad, white, decided—it pointed to the north. At this moment of my midnight walk, to have had my head suddenly pulled back and the gleam of a razor flashed across my eyes would not have surprised me. "Jack the Ripper" was in the air. I stood still and looked round with apprehension, nobody, not a footstep, only the sound of a distant cab. I walked quietly across Oxford Street. There was the confounded thing, against the doll shop, bright, shining, pointing straight ahead. I crossed over into Charlotte Street. There it was again, at the side of the house of Forbes Robertson. I felt a temptation, a dreadful curiosity, I must follow it, and went on opposite and past the house where I lived, on till I came to the Square, crossed over to the enclosure, and then, close to the railings, there it was again, palpable, commanding. " Come," it said, "follow." Then suddenly I got a panic and ran back, fancying a step behind me, ran back as fast as my legs would carry me, to No. —, and, standing on the doorstep, breathless, shaking and trembling, had the unspeakable happiness of hearing the mellifluous voice of the celebrated Bessie, making the equally celebrated inquiry, "Wot cheer,' Ria?" What could the arrow have meant? Somehow, I felt that night I had been very close to a rat-trap.

CHAPTER XXXII.

1886—In New York with the McCaul company—"Josephine sold by her Sisters"—Mrs. Brown Potter and Mrs. Langtry—Bishop Potter of New York—His views of the stage—The McCaul company—Eugene Oudin—Miss Louise Parker—The marriage of "Gene" and Louise—Married at midnight in her stage dress—I give her away—Chicago in 1887—The anarchists in gaol—A visit to the condemned men—A picturesque bomb-thrower—The gaol arrangements—Behind the iron bars—Mr. and Mrs. Parsons—"Annie Laurie"—The execution—The funeral—Encore "Annie Laurie"—The mourning multitudes—Chicago under concealed surveillance—Not a drink for forty-eight hours.

In July, 1886, I sailed for New York, under contract to Colonel McCaul to play in "Josephine-sold by her Sisters." On the steamer was an elderly gentleman whose name I did not know. But we used to talk—talk about theatres, too. "What do you think of the relative artistic claims of Mrs. Brown Potter and Mrs. Langtry?" said he one day. "Well," said I, "I think Mrs. Brown Potter has more dramatic instinct in her little finger than Mrs. Langtry has in her whole body." "I am very glad to hear you say so," replied the gentleman. "I am Bishop Potter of New York, a relation of Mrs. Brown Potter, and though I don't exactly hold with her adopting the stage, still I hold that what is worth doing, is worth doing well, and I say again I am glad to hear you think she has, in your opinion, a chance of success."

During my engagement with the McCaul company, I met one of the most interesting artists I have ever known—Eugene Oudin, whose early death in November, 1894, was a distinct loss to art, and a dreadful misfortune to all who loved him. The prima donna of the company was a young American lady, Miss Louise Parker, of Providence, Rhode Island, just returned from Paris, where she had studied with Mme. Merchesi and Mme. La Grange; the tenor was Signor Perugini, an American of Italian extraction and a very popular singer in the States. He made his first public appearance when very young, as a baby, at a "baby show;" he was successful, and won a prize. Perugini took more pains and time in his "make up" than any artist I ever knew, and once upon a time told me, with conscious pride, that he used ninety-six several pigments in the process. Some two or three years ago he had the happiness of becoming the husband of the lovely Miss Lilian Russell—fine artiste, magnificent woman, and the pet of the American public from the Atlantic to the Pacific.

Mr. De Wolf Hopper was the principal comedian; and among the chorus was a bright, sparkling, pretty, piquante little brunette, who had a wonderful contralto voice. Her name was Miss May Yohe, now Lady Francis Hope.

Eugene Oudin was of a modest disposition, and always considered he could not act. To tell the truth, at this time, September, 1886, his histrionic gifts were not great, but his voice was beautiful and his method perfect.

He was a prejudiced boy, prejudiced in my favour, thought I knew everything about the stage, and begged me to watch him from the side and tell him where he was "dreadful" and "would I help him to alter it." And I did, and after a bit Louise came and looked and criticised him too. After the New York season we travelled, our ultimate destination being Chicago.

On this journey, in the different theatres Miss Parker and I shared the same dressing-room, and somehow it did not seem long before we two, between ourselves, got to talk about "Gene." Then in a little time she told me they were "engaged," and one Saturday, in Detroit, after the matinée, "Gene" electrified me by asking,

"Would I give Louise away? They were going to be married that very night, after the performance." And so they were. The bride was married in the stage costume she had been playing in. It was all very sudden and delightful, and I, like an idiot, cried my eyes out. You see I had no experience, had never been a bridesmaid, and only once a bride. The only wedding I had ever attended was my own (a runaway one). There was a terrible dearth of wedding presents. De Wolf Hopper, by superhuman and wonderful means, got some silver forks and spoons. And I—I had some Australian nuggets in my dressing-bag, and I sent one to the bride: "A piece of virgin gold, emblematic of herself." We had some supper and champagne, and at 2 a.m. the bride and groom and the bridal company boarded the train for Chicago—Westward Ho. Everybody said "Gene" was to be a great artist, and his subsequent career justified their opinion. Seldom has a finer performance been seen than his Sir Brian de Bois Guilbert in Sir Arthur Sullivan's Opera of "Ivanhoe," produced at the Royal English Opera House, January 31st, 1891.

In the fall of 1887 I was again in Chicago. At this time the anarchists lay under sentence of death for dynamite outrage and murder of policemen in the Haymarket. Their counsel, Colonel Black, had gone to Washington or New York, I forget which, to move the Supreme Court to try to get the sentences altered, or the prisoners respited. I had a great desire to see the men, and by the exercise of some Press influence succeeded in getting into the prison when the general public were excluded.

I was taken through a small room, where warders, keepers, and other officials were lounging on tables and chairs round the stove, smoking, talking, laughing, and jesting, into an immense lofty stone hall or corridor, down the centre of which was an iron grating, extending the whole length of the chamber, and reaching from the floor to the ceiling—the sort of grating one sees in front of the lion's den. Behind this grating were two rows of cells, one above the other, the condemned cells, two tiers, communicating with each other by a flight of iron steps. While I stood looking, down the steps from the upper tier ran one of the handsomest young men I have ever seen. He was in his shirt sleeves, a white shirt wide open at the throat, and under the rolling collar was a blood-red silk handkerchief, tied loosely in a broad bow, with flowing ends. His sleeves were turned up to the elbow, and his arms were white and strong, his trousers were pulled in tight to the waist with a broad strap, for he wore no braces. He was fair, with a profusion of long, bright, waving, chestnut hair thrown off the forehead. His eyes were blue, fearless, and bright, and he ran down the steps smiling, and smoking a big cigar. In his hand was an empty basket, and as he reached the grating, a woman, with a basket of fine fruit, pushed past me. The officer on duty unlocked a door in the grating, the baskets were exchanged, the door relocked, and the woman and the smiling prisoner stood laughing and talking through the bars. They spoke German. Presently a man came along, and gave him (through the bars) a handful of big cigars. The condemned anarchists numbered six, but somehow the others did not impress me, only this one, and one other, Parsons, a mean, dark, pallid, dingy person, wearing a greasy frock coat, who was looking anxiously at the door by which I had entered. Sometimes he stood grasping the iron bars, and, laying his pale face against them, rested and waited. Then he would walk up and down, up and down. Then, stopping, he grasped the bars, shaking them violently, like a wild thing. At last, arrives what he is waiting for—a man and a woman, both deadly pale. The man halts, and stops to speak to an inquiring officer, to whose question he replies by a shake of the head. The woman, thin, mean, sallow, ascetic, dressed in shabby black, beckons Parsons. They both go down to the end of the corridor, down, out of earshot, but one can see, and to save my life, I cannot help it, I have to look. She puts her arms through the bars, and takes him by the shoulders. He does the same to her, they press their faces close, and kiss each other, once, twice, thrice; then she sighs, and rests her face sideways on the bars. And the man stands back a bit, looks up, and is, if possible, more deadly white than before. ' Who are they?" I ask the officer. "The man is Parsons, the anarchist, and the woman is his wife. Colonel Black, their counsel, is just back from Washington." " No hope?" said I. " No," said he.

Within a day or two the six criminals were executed; they were all hung just round the corner of the corridor (a bungling business, the ropes went wrong), but not before my blonde friend had spoilt his beauty by trying to blow himself up with a dynamite cartridge, got from goodness knows where.

On the night before the execution, one of the prisoners woke the whole jail, and made hardened sinners weep and cry and sob, by starting to sing, at 1 a.m., in a lovely tenor voice, "Annie Laurie." They hanged them on a Saturday, their bodies were given to their friends, who conveyed the remains to "Undertaking Parlours," and all Chicago took a farewell look. They were buried on Sunday, taken to their graves, covered with mantles of white flowers. Each hearse was accompanied by a brass band, and as the procession passed my hotel the strains of "Annie Laurie" mingled with the tramp of many feet, and the moan of muffled drums stole along, slow and sad. No wonder the tears ran down the cheeks of the waiting multitudes, men and women alike. Who, hearing and seeing, could help it? I couldn't.

At the time of these executions, Chicago was a city of many terrors. The grip of the law was on her throat, thousands of soldiers were concealed in various buildings. The cellars of many blocks round the prison were filled with the police. The theatres were open, but the saloons were closed. Not a drink to be got for forty-eight hours.

CHAPTER XXXIII.

Meeting with Mrs. Boucicault in Louisville, 1887—New York in 1888—Sophie Eyre—Where she is buried—A matinée at Wallack's—Mr. Dion Boucicault and his new wife—The last days of Selina Dolaro—Mrs. Boucicault kindly supplies me with material for a Boucicault chapter—Mr. Boucicault at the Lyceum Theatre with his son Willie in 1869.

In 1887 in Louisville I had the pleasure of making the personal acquaintance of Mrs. Dion Boucicault and her little dog, such a pretty black-and-tan King Charles. We were two lonely Englishwomen staying at the same hotel, The Galt House, and naturally had much to talk about.

At the end of the season everybody gravitates to New York, and it was there, in 1888, I renewed a friendship with one of the most charming women I ever met, Sophie Eyre. Beautiful she was in my eyes, and with an attraction about her (for me) that up to this moment I cannot exactly understand or explain. She was staying in Brooklyn at the finest hotel, where nothing would do but

I must come over quite often, and she entertained me like an empress. Fruit, flowers, choice dishes, unique wines, nothing was too good or too expensive for her guest. Poor Sophie. She sleeps her last sleep at Capri, lulled by the musical murmuring seas of the Medi terre.

In New York, too, I again met Mrs. Boucicault, this time accompanied by her son Aubrey. One day we three went to a matinée at Wallack's. We sat in the front row of the stalls. Presently Mrs. Dion nudged me. "Look there," said she, lifting her eyes to a box just above us on my left. In the box were seated Mr. Dion Boucicault and his new wife, Louise Thorndyke Boucicault. We were very close, and could have shaken hands all round, but we didn't. About this time Mrs. Boucidault and I went to see Selina Dolaro. She was living in 24th Street—had some millinery parlours there. She was looking delicate and fragile; but was not badly off, having recently had a benefit, got up by the "Lambs' Club" of New York, at which something like 4000 dols. was cleared. The idea was to send her to Florida to recuperate, but she would not go. "Rather die in New York," said she, "than live in Florida." She was gay and bright, and walked down Broadway a bit with us. The next day I sailed for

England, and three weeks after poor Dolly was dead.

Mrs. Dion Boucicault has kindly given me many interesting items of her own career, also of Mr. Boucicault's—two lives, as she herself says, full of romance and adventure.

Mr. Boucicault to me personally was always a most interesting man. The first time I saw him (except when he was acting) was one morning at the Lyceum, during the "Chilperic" season. We were rehearsing, and through the door from the stalls came Mr. Boucicault and his son Willie. The father, wearing an Inverness cape thrown back from the shoulders, had his left arm round the neck of his son. I said to him afterwards, "How fond you are of that boy." "Yes," he replied; "if anything happened to him I should die."

CHAPTER XXXIV.

Mr. Boucicault—Where born—His family originally from Tours—His father—His mother cousin to present Lord Chief Justice of New South Wales—Where I first saw Mr. and Mrs. Boucicault—First appearance of Miss Marie Litton—The genesis of the "Colleen Bawn"—Its production—The original cast—The "Colleen" in London—The Queen at the theatre—The Queen's appreciation of Mr. and Mrs. Boucicault—The Princess Alice—Production of the "Octoroon," New York, 1859, the day John Brown was hung—Public excitement—Threats to shoot Mrs. Boucicault—The piece—Revised by the public—Production of "Arrah na Pogue," Princess's Theatre—The Clerkenwell explosion—The Prince of Wales and Mr. Boucicault.

MR. BOUCICAULT was born in Lower Gardiner Street, Dublin, 1822, and was the son of Samuel Boucicault. The family were originally of Tours in the South of France, but on the Revocation of the Edict of Nantes, they emigrated to Ireland, finally settling in Dublin. His mother was the beautiful Miss Darley, cousin of the now Sir Frederick Darley, Lord Chief Justice of Sydney, N.S.W.

"Do you know the first time I saw you both on the stage?" said I, interrupting. "It was at the

Princess's, in 'Jeannie Deans.' Your hair was parted in the centre, and your feet—I thought the most beautiful feet I had ever seen—were bare." " No," said she, " they were not bare. I wore canvas ballet shoes, loosely bound, so they should not mark the side of the foot; over them were drawn silk fleshings, on which were traced the outlines of the toes: the effect was perfect. Yes," she went on, musingly, "Mr. Boucicault was Counsel for the Defence, and Miss Marie Litton made her first appearance on the stage as Effie Deans. Dion coached her in the part."

During our conversation, I learnt that "The Colleen Bawn," produced at the Olympic Theatre, New York, 1858 or 1859, under the management of the celebrated Laura Keene, was an experiment, and the first Irish drama written by Dion Boucicault.

The run of " Jeannie Deans " had been wonderfully successful, and much money had been made. After that came " Vanity Fair," an adaptation from the French, by Mr. Boucicault. It was a failure, and after a managerial consultation there was a talk of closing the theatre. Mrs. Boucicault suggested that as the Scotch drama had gone so well, why not write an Irish piece. But Dion did not believe in Irish drama, and said, " No." After the consultation, walking up Broadway on their way to the hotel, they passed a second-hand bookstall. It was in the basement at the bottom of five or six steps. Dion liked hunting second-hand bookstalls, so down he went, and Mrs. Boucicault waited at the top. After a few minutes, holding a book up, he asked, "Do you know anything about this?" "What is it?" said Mrs. Boucicault. "Gerald Griffin's 'Collegians,'" answered Mr. Boucicault. "Don't know much about it," was the reply, "but I think it is founded on the ballad of 'Willie Riley and his Colleen Bawn.'" "Well, I'll have it," said Dion, paying the price, ten cents.

He read the book that afternoon, and remarked, "I think I can make something of this." "You see," said Mrs. Boucicault, "he saw me as the Colleen Bawn from the very beginning."

That night, after the theatre, Mrs. Boucicault, tired to death, threw herself on the outside of the bed, and Dion, sitting down to his desk, made notes and scenario of the first act. By twelve next day the scene plots were in the theatre. The piece was written, rehearsed, and produced in nine days, and made a tremendous hit.

The "dive" and "rescue" were not in the

original drama, but were added after a week or two. In the New York cast were :—

Anne Chute	Miss Laura Keene.
The Colleen Bawn	Miss Agnes Robertson.
Sheda	Miss Mary Wells.
Myles na Coppaleen	Mr. D. Boucicault.
Danny Man	Mr. Charles Wheatley.
Corrigan	Mr. Burnett.
Father Tom	Mr. Dan Leeson.

Mr. Dan Leeson came over with the Boucicaults, and was the original Father Tom here.

When "The Colleen Bawn" was produced at the Adelphi Theatre, London, September 10th, 1860, it repeated the New York furore. The Queen was so delighted she went three times in one fortnight, and was in the theatre when she got the news of the (subsequently fatal) illness of the Duchess of Kent. She took such an interest in the play that the expedition to Killarney was the direct consequence.

A special copy of the drama was by request made for her Majesty, with the pictures of "Myles na Coppaleen" and his "Colleen Bawn." The Princess Alice appropriating this, another one had to be made for the Queen.

Corbould, the Royal Academician, "by command" painted in oil the portraits of Mr. and

Mrs. Boucicault, and they were hung in Windsor Castle. "And where are they now?" said I. "Why, hanging there still, I suppose," said Mrs. Boucicault.

"The Octoroon" was produced at the Winter Garden, New York, Dec. 2nd, 1859, on the very night John Brown was hung. There was plenty of excitement attending the first performance. New York was up in arms against the Southerners and their peculiar institution. The idea was abhorrent to them, and threats were made that if Mrs. Boucicault dared to stand up in the slave scene to be sold, she would be shot on sight. But she did dare, looking lovely all in white. The theatre was packed with police, and Mrs. Boucicault still lives to tell the tale.

The piece was an enormous success. Men, women, and girls sat and cried and sobbed their hearts out, without any idea of concealing their emotions. The play originally ended with Zoë dying, poisoned. But the public would not stand that, and insisted that she should "live," so the author wrote another act, and announced "The Octoroon," "written by Dion Boucicault and revised by the public to whom it is dedicated."

Here is the original cast :—

Salem Scudder	Joe J. Jefferson.
McClosky	J. B. Johnston.
Wah no tee	Dion Boucicault.
Guy Paton	Dolly Davenport.
Pete	— Jamieson.
Zoë	Miss Agnes Robertson.

"Arrah na Pogue," the third of this celebrated cycle was, by a strange coincidence, produced at the Princess's Theatre, London, on the very night of the Clerkenwell explosion, December 13th, 1867. It had been arranged to sing in it "The wearing of the Green," but on hearing of the dreadful catastrophe they substituted "Shan van Voght." The Prince of Wales was present at the production, and after the performance went round to Mr. Boucicault's dressing-room, and while sitting on a table, smoking a cigar, said, " Boucicault, are you a Fenian ? " Dion replied, " No, sir, I am not a Fenian, but I am an Irishman."

CHAPTER XXXV.

Miss Agnes Robertson as an Infant Prodigy—Her first appearances—Plays Tyrone Power's parts—The first person to dance the polka in Dublin—Comes to London—A member of the Princess's company—Resides with Mr. and Mrs. Charles Kean—The young actress a particular favourite with the Queen—Mr. Charles Kean—The "Master of the Revels"—The Queen always gay and laughing—The Prince Consort grave and dignified—A royal visit to the Princess's Theatre—Mr. Emden receives her Majesty—A terrible fall—Three little maids looking through a fanlight—What they saw—A dramatic incident in the private life of Mr. and Mrs. Boucicault.

MISS AGNES ROBERTSON was an "infant prodigy." She did not like the title, neither did her maternal grandfather, the Rev. Dr. Dunsmore-Muir, Grand Master of the St. Mary's and Kilwinning Lodge of Freemasons, Professor of Greek, Hebrew, and Astronomy at the High School of Edinburgh. At a testimonial concert given to Morris Barnett, the well-known musician and composer, in the Free Trade Hall, Newcastle-on-Tyne, a tiny girl stood on a stool and sang, " Love is a mischievous boy," and made such a sensation, that she was offered a professional engagement, which was accepted. The tiny one was Agnes Robertson, and at Aberdeen, when she was ten years old, she played her first part, "The spoilt Child," for the benefit of Mr. Ryder, the manager of the Theatre Royal, who had been mentally afflicted. Afterwards she visited Glasgow, Belfast, then on to Dublin, playing Tyrone Power's parts, Paddy Murphy, in "The Happy Man," and Dr. O'Toole in "The Irish Tutor," and singing in costume, between the acts, "The Ladies' Man." She stayed in Dublin, studying ballet dancing, with Mme. Duelin, and was the first person to dance the "polka" in that city. Mr. and Mrs. Charles Kean took a great fancy to her. She came to London, lived with them, and became a member of the Princess's company. She was always a particular favourite with the Queen.

Mr. Charles Kean, being "Master of the Revels," superintended all the performances at the Castle, but the "casts" were invariably submitted for the Royal approval. One day, her Majesty, on looking over the proposed bill, said, "Well, but Mr. Kean, where is little Miss Robertson? I don't see her name." Mr. Kean explained that the piece was not being performed by the Princess's company. "Never mind that," said the Queen, "you must put her in, we like her to be always included." Mrs.

Boucicault said in those days the Queen was always gay and laughing, but the Prince Consort was grave and dignified.

One night, on the occasion of a Royal visit to the Princess's, a very funny incident occurred. When Charles Kean was not in the bill he received her Majesty himself, but when he was playing, this duty devolved on the acting manager, Mr. Emden.

In order to get to the Royal box, one had to walk down a long corridor, and then to ascend some five or six treacherous steps. Opening on to this corridor, close to the steps, was the fanlight of one of the dressing-rooms. In this dressing-room, on the evening of the Royal visit, were three girls—Lottie Leclerq, Polly Keeley, and Agnes Robertson. When the Royal party came along, the three girls clambered on a table and peeped through the fanlight. The sight of their acting manager, carrying two candles, and walking backwards up the steps, of which he was naturally nervous, proved too much for the peeping girls. They began to giggle audibly, and vainly trying to stifle the sound of their giggles, they snorted loudly. Mr. Emden was overwhelmed with dismay, missed his footing and sat down on the top step in the presence of her Majesty, covered with confusion and candle-grease. The Queen, following Emden's gaze, lifted her eyes to the fanlight, and discovering the culprits, pointed them out to the Prince Consort, and leaning against the wall, laughed long and loudly. But his Royal Highness was shocked at such levity, and looked it.

Mrs. Boucicault related to me a very dramatic incident in her private life. It was a Saturday night, the last night of the "Shaughran" at the "Princess's." Her son Willie had a few days before left London to visit some friends in the country. His father was to buy him a farm "out West," and the boy had gone down to Huntingdonshire to pick up agricultural points. On this particular Saturday Mrs. Boucicault fancied there was something strange in the manner of the people about her, and no newspapers came to the house, but did not take much notice. At night, near the end of the performance, she saw her brother-in-law standing in the wings, looking very white and distressed. Then she saw him talking to Dion. After the curtain was down Mr. Boucicault said: "I am going *directly*, the carriage will come back for you." In her dressing-room was Emily Muir, looking dreadfully ill. "What's the matter?" asked Mrs. Boucicault. "Nothing," said Emily; "I don't feel quite well." "I wonder," said Mrs. Boucicault, "what," naming her brother-in-law, " was behind for? and, fancy, Dion has taken the carriage. I sha'n't wait; come along, we'll have a cab." They went home to Regent Street. When the door opened she found the hall full of servants and people. " What is it ? " said she; but nobody answered. She ran upstairs, and in the drawing-room found her brother-in-law and Dion. Dion was sitting on a couch, his head buried in his hands. " What's the matter?" Nobody answered. "I know something's the matter with Willie. Something has happened. Where's the carriage? I must go to him at once." Dion started up, and shaking his right hand at her, cried out violently: " You can't go to him, woman. He is dead."

CHAPTER XXXVI.

At Salem, Massachusetts—In the graveyard.

IN the autumn of 1889 I was at Salem, Massachusetts, for a day or two. The town was to me full of weird interest, as being not only the birthplace of Nathaniel Hawthorne, the author of the "Scarlet Letter," but also the headquarters of the "Witchfinders" in those dead and gone but unforgotten devilish days of which we have all heard and read so much.

Of course the "*de*-pôt," as our cousins call the railway station, was right up-to-date, full of American go and bustle, but five minutes' walk brought you into a sleepy old English town one hundred years behind the times.

In Salem there is a delightful old English inn, the "Essex," with stabling and long sheds where the country carts were put up on market days, and loose boxes for the horses. They are all empty now, but I am told that at night you can hear the munching of ghostly steeds getting away with any amount of ghostly "wuts," and ghostly gnawings and nibblings of material mangers, and any doubting Thomas can see the *marks* in the morning; but irreverent ones shake their heads and murmur "rats," which is a very comprehensive term in the States. After lunch, which is dinner in these primitive parts, I go on a pilgrimage "down town," the great feature of which, I am given to understand, is the "Natural History Museum," pronounced "*muse*-em," and which, I am gravely informed, is "well worth seeing." Its situation (over a third-rate tailor's store) rather detracts from its dignity. But on the other hand the side of the door bears a legend setting forth that "This museum was bought and done up" ("done up" is superfluous, one can see it at a glance) "and presented to the city of Salem by George Peabody." With the memory of the Peabody millions crowding one's mind, the "muse-em" seems rather a one-horse show for such a Monte Cristo to set upon its (last) legs. Up you go, up one flight of worm-eaten and foot-worn stairs, and enter the sanctuary. It is a long, low, narrow room, with a row of prehistoric cases down the centre. At either end are large old-fashioned windows, the front ones looking on the principal street of Salem, the back ones are made shady and beautiful with graceful waving trees. There is nobody there and nothing to see, except a few faded whales' bones, and a few cases of moth-eaten birds, decorated with a camphory smell, much dust, and the transparent pale bodies of defunct flies. Half way up the room you happen upon a moth-eaten old man—the janitor, I suppose. With difficulty and many weary wheezes, he pulls himself out of a deep-seated, moth-eaten old chair. "Anythin' I ken dew fer yew, *mam?*" "No, thank you," say I. "Here's a fine specimen of a mummy," coughs he. "It's thousands an' thousands of years old. It's not quite complete, but I reckon it's about the finest mummy in the world," says this breathless and toothless and shameless old gentleman, with a smack of his trembling old lips. "Is that so?" say I. "Well, I think I've seen finer ones in the British Museum." "Why, yes, *mam*," says he slowly, and blinking at me with his pink-edged and rheumy eyes; "of course I meant in the *new* world, *mam*; yes, yes, yes," he goes on, rubbing his hands slowly. "I've bin in th' British Museum. Why, I've bin ter London six times, an' allers went ter the Museum every time. I was a ship's cap'en an' used ter board close ter Paul's Church, an' when I wasn't in th' Muse-em or the ship, I was in Paul's Church. Ah! they was rare times. An' I was young then—young, young." And he sank down in his chair in a tired sort of way. But he was a cheery old chap, and after a minute turned over his "chaw" with renewed satisfaction, and expectoration. I told him I was English, and wanted to see "The house with the seven gables." "Ah, yes," he says; "but it's a mort of a way," and with a mighty effort he pulled himself again out of the moth-eaten chair. "You want ter see old things, an' old places; come this way." And we went to the window where the trees waved; he opened it, and we looked almost directly over a graveyard. The old man stretched out his arm, "You see there," said he, "that's the oldest graveyard in Massachusetts; you see that house in the corner, the one with the rotten, falling-down green shutters, eh? yes? Well, that is Dr. Grimshaw's house. You recollect the story, 'Dr. Grimshaw's Secret'?" I nodded. "Well, *he*, Nathaniel, married the doctor's daughter, an' that's where they lived, an' that's where th' story's laid." I thanked him, and, following his directions, "down a narrow street by the side of the museum," presently find myself at the graveyard. You go in at a little white side gate, and the click of the falling latch sounds strangely familiar. Why, the scene is English, quite English, full of trees, such old, old trees, and the chilly and moaning winds creep sadly through them, the dry leaves rustle and rattle, and drop slowly and wistfully and reluctantly to the ground; there are little heaps of yellow and brown and faded red ones, drifted against the sheltering corners of the crooked and leaning and mossy gravestones, which the tall, rank, tawny and grey coarse grass (tall as harvest ripe wheat) clasps so closely, so lovingly, and to me there seems a movement and a shiver among them, as I, a stranger in the land, intrude on this domain, " Sacred to the memory of . . . " There is an immense old oak, originally brought from England; under it is a slab of stone, on which the minister used to stand to read the Burial Service. What generations of ministers must have stood upon it; it is quite worn in the centre.

Out of the silent distant past comes the memory of a grass-grown graveyard in the Midlands, and the words of the minister, bright and clear, " I am the Resurrection and the Life," " Whoso believeth in Me shall never die." Again I am a little child—in the days when they did not decorate the graves with wreaths and flowers, only with the tears and sighs of the mourners.

The broken windows of the doctor's deserted house look upon the Ministers' Oak.

There are lots of people from England buried in this Salem graveyard. Some of the inscriptions go as far back as 1600, long before the witch days. There is the grave of a young mother who died about that time, " aged 21 years," and the next day her baby died, " aged 24 hours." It seems to me a wonderful thing that this sculptured fact should stare me in the face after all these years. Near the principal gate, and on each side of the principal pathway (now grass-grown), are five or six large, oblong stone tombs, about four feet high, and topped with a heavy slab and cornice. The names are not legible, but the dates are. The first one is 1690, then follows 1695, 1697, 1699. I suppose the boys in those days were much like the boys in these, and no doubt demure little Puritans played marbles on the tops of these convenient sarcophagi. But there is no frivolity of that kind now. The place is closed except to "visitors," and "dogs are not admitted." But with that fine disregard of the city ordinance, which characterises most people and things in many places besides the United States, the Salem city dog lies flat on his stomach, creeps under the gate and runs around "sniffing" in a doggy manner and behaving in a doggy fashion. There was one engaged in active investigation when I arrived; he knew he had no business there, and looked at me with a deprecating "don't you tell" sort of expression (we were the only visitors present), then he hung his head—and his tail—bent his back, and, slipping out under the gate, fled for his life. You are also requested "not to walk on the grass," but as the grass flourishes plentifully in every possible place, it is difficult to avoid walking on it. I picked up an acorn from "The Ministers' Oak," and putting on the list slippers of a vicarious grief, stole out in that quiet way one naturally adopts when coming from a graveyard. Why should people affect to be so sad at a "transition," which in its heavenly rewards is to make amends for every *earthly* bliss we have missed or been done out of? Why?

CHAPTER XXXVII.

How many times I have been arrested in the States—What it costs—How to travel comfortably in America—The best hiding places on board ship—What it costs—The Denver quarantine—Barnes Station—And how I was taken for Mrs. O'Shea.

TRAVELLING in the States, especially for public people, is full of possibilities, but fuller of sheriffs.

I have been arrested on "put-up" claims, "breach of contract," the usual pretext, in nearly every State of the Union, and it generally cost 100 dols. to convince the officer the thing was a mistake. To travel comfortably in America, one must have nothing, and give it to someone else to mind. I have been locked up in the bullion room of an Atlantic liner by a purser, who has now joined the majority. I have been behind the door of a large empty cabin at the extreme end of a big steamship, the door held firmly back by the polite chief steward, while three sheriffs' officers glanced round. "Nothin' here. I guess this is the last cabin, ain't it, steward?" "That's so, gentlemen," locking the door behind him. I am locked in, and safe. This "touch and go" job cost 50 dols.—25 dols. to the chief steward, 25 dols. to the chief stewardess. I have had two offers of marriage on the cars, the would-be bridegroom, in one case, offering to find a parson on board the train, and have the thing settled "right away." I have been as nearly as possible "side tracked" by the handsomest cow-boy in Arizona, Colonel Charles Spencer. I have been "snowed in" at Truckee, and "washed out" on the Plains. I have lunched on the summit of the Rockies, and mailed a post-card (which was safely delivered) to London from the summit of the Sierras. I have been down a silver mine in Virginia City, where the temperature was so high you had to take a hot bath before returning to the surface, and I have been up a mountain in the same locality an hour later, gathering ice to eat with the strawberries just arrived from 'Frisco. I have eaten bear's pad in St. Louis, and been introduced to native and growling lions at Green River.

Talking of Green River recalls to me the Denver quarantine. Green River is a mountain station, and derives its name, presumably, from the total absence of anything that could possibly be mistaken for a river, green, or otherwise. Going east from 'Frisco, in the fall of 1890, we stopped at Green River for breakfast, and to take on the cars from the north-west, timed to arrive about 10 a.m. But they did not do so till 6 p.m., and then we found they had been delayed by a sensation. Somewhere between Portland, Oregon, and Green River, a boy was taken ill. At the first possible place a doctor was fetched, who diagnosed the case as "small-pox," and the authorities of that city would not allow him to be removed from the coach, which, with all the people travelling in it, was placed at the tail of the train, the doors locked, guards placed outside at each end, and no one allowed in or out. We left Green River about 8 p.m., the infected car still being placed last. Next day, about noon, when some forty or fifty or sixty miles from Denver, in the middle of a vast and sandy plain, the train came to a standstill, and, as the custom is, the men got out, and began popping at the prairie dogs. But the prairie dogs were more than seven, and simultaneously with the pull of the trigger, the tiny ones, frisking their pretty tails, disappeared into their holes. After about twenty minutes' waiting and some shouting, there was a cry, "All aboard," and off we went. Then someone said, "Why, we've left a car on the track." Everybody rushed to look. It was true enough. The small-pox car was standing on a little siding, the guards were withdrawn, and the doors were evidently locked, for the men, frantic, were jumping out of the windows, shaking their fists and swearing. Of course they were swearing, you could see it, and one man fired his revolver, but we soon lost sight of them. I asked the conductor what was the meaning of it. He said the Denver authorities would not allow the small-pox car within so many miles of the city, that the people were "quarantined." "Well, about provisions, what will they do?" "A car will be sent along to-night and each morning with a doctor and everything required. The things will be set down on the prairie at a distance, and the passengers will fetch them into the coach." " And how long will they be kept there?" "Two or three weeks, probably. When the doctor certifies the city it is safe, everything in the car will be burned, the car and the people fumigated, disinfected, and the passengers, supplied with fresh clothing, will resume their journey."

When we arrived at Denver the place was alive with excitement, and big Press boards announced:

"THE SMALL-POX CLAMOURING AT OUR GATES."

"THE SMALL-POX FIEND IS ABROAD."

"DEADLY, DISGUSTING DISEASE."

"DEATH IN THE DESERT."

And that is how they "quarantine" in, or rather outside, Denver.

On my return to England, in 1891, I had an odd experience. I stayed with my sister, at "The Cottage," Mill Hill, Barnes Common. I went frequently to London, and the officials at the Barnes Station were more than uncommonly polite; they carried my little parcel or my umbrella across the bridge, they got my ticket, a porter was always at hand to open the carriage door. I certainly had never before met with such attention, and such a touching of caps, and I appreciated it, more especially after so much experience of travel in the States, where one always has to do and carry everything for one's self, and nobody ever touches their cap. One day at the station bookstall I ordered a lot of papers, among them an illustrated one containing a portrait (from a photo) of Mrs. O'Shea, of which I bought four copies, intending to send one to the *San Francisco Examiner,* which, during the excitement of the O'Shea-Parnell episode, had published as a "portrait of Mrs. O'Shea" a reproduction of a flamboyant "hair-restored" lady, with no clothes on to speak of, only her golden hair was hanging down her back, and the original of which, to my certain knowledge, had been in the front row of the ballet. I told the man to send the papers over to "The Cottage," and went on my way to London. When I returned, my sister showed me the packet of papers; they were directed to "Mrs. O'Shea."

"What does this mean?" said she.

"Not the slightest idea," said I.

Off trotted Clara across the common to the station.

"What do you mean by this?" said she, showing the man the direction.

"That's right," said he. "The lady told me to send them to 'The Cottage.'"

"What lady?"

"Mrs. O'Shea."

"Mrs. O'Shea, indeed; that's not Mrs. O'Shea; that's my sister, Mme. Emily Soldene."

The man was profuse in his apologies. "Everybody on the station thought the lady was Mrs. O'Shea."

But alas! for me, the spell was broken; no more extraordinary attention, no more exceptional touching of caps. In the immediate future I carried my umbrella and my small parcel myself, unnoticed, through the crowd.

I afterwards heard that Mrs. O'Shea was staying with a relative lower down the line, and that was how the mistake arose, and my dearest friends said, " Well, you certainly are like her."

To tell the truth, I was always very much taken with Charles Stewart Parnell myself, and could have wished the " Uncrowned King " had perceived and been impressed with the resemblance.

CHAPTER XXXVIII.

My ideas on the privileges enjoyed by artistes—An experience among the "residuum"—The Queen and Prince on Thanksgiving Day—Sir John Bennett and his cocked hat—Another experience among the "residuum"—London music-halls as contrasted with Australia and America—How I came to write—Charles Dickens and my father-in-law—To my readers, "good-bye," or "au revoir"—Which?

I HAVE often thought that one of the chiefest charms of an artist's life is the personal feeling and recognition, not to say a kind of affection, one gets from the public, more particularly among the lower classes. The singer or player is always bound up in their pleasantest memories, when the cares and troubles were laid aside, and everybody was going to have a good time. It has been my privilege to earn the applause of all ranks, from their Royal Highnesses the Prince and Princess of Wales to the coster and his wife of Whitechapel. And let me take this opportunity of saying that my art has been, and still is, the one great delight of my life; and in whatever direction engaged, or whatever the grade of the audience, I have been always the same. I gave them the best of my ability and all my heart and soul, and could do no more.

But to return to "personal feeling." When the Prince of Wales went to St. Paul's in 1872 (the Thanksgiving), I had a seat engaged for me in a first floor over a shop close to old Temple Bar, on the north side of Fleet Street. I forget if it was the fish shop or the hairdresser's. The side door opened on to an alley way that you could enter from some little distance up Chancery Lane. The crush was awful, and I soon was separated from my party. When I got into the alley I found myself in the midst of a dense mass of people, you could not move or breathe. I felt I should be torn to pieces, or drop and be trampled under foot. "'Old hup, missus; wot's th' matter? you're hall right," said a rough-looking man. "I can't bear it," I gasped, "I—am afraid." "'Ere, look a 'ere, Bill, 'ere's a lark; th' gal's hafraid." Bill looked at me, then suddenly burst out, "Blow me hif hit hain't Miss Soldene hat the 'Phil.' Don't yer know me, miss? Wy, hi 'as my wilk barrer houtside ev'ry night. W'ere d'yer want ter go, miss?" I told him. "Wot, that little door hin th' wall hover there? That's hall right. 'Ere, boys, giv hus er 'and." And before I could get my breath, five or six rough men were round me and I was in the doorway safe and sound—got my little seat in the little first floor, and saw the sight, too—Her Most Gracious Majesty, in black silk and miniver, and by her side H.R.H., bareheaded, bowing, bowing, all the time. And soon, to our sorrow, we saw he was also baldheaded. How the people shouted and screamed, and hanging on to every possible place, hurrahed themselves hoarse; and the guns boomed, and the bells clashed and clanged; and Sir John Bennett, looking handsome and debonair, rode a big spirited white horse that capered, and curvetted, and volted and demi-volted, and stood on his hind legs, nearly throwing off Sir John, and quite throwing off Sir John's cocked hat. But the watchmaker of Cheapside sat firm like a knight of old, and his beautiful wavy white hair streamed out on the breeze and glittered and shone like spun glass in the bright sun; and didn't the people cheer when he resumed his gay and glorious and unaccustomed headgear, and Sir John, who was of a merry humour, raised it again and again, saluting his cheerers and laughing outright.

Another time, coming from the theatre alone in a four-wheel cab through the Seven Dials, a pitch-dark night, late and raining, the man driving furiously, the cab swaying from side to side, the horse stumbled and fell, the cab seemed to run over on to his back, and he began to kick. It was just at the entrance of one of those dark courts which at that time abounded in the neighbourhood. Out rushed a lot of people, dreadful-looking men and women. They opened the cab door, and I alighted. There was a lamp hanging in the sort of archway leading up the court. "Wy, hit's Miss Soldene," said one of the dirty women. "Don't you mind, miss, hi'm one o' th' cleaners hat th' 'Lambra. Hit's hall right; stand 'ere hout o' th' rain; pull yer cloak hup close an' cover hup yer dimants," said she in a whisper. "Yes," said the other women crowding round, "you're hall right, we'll see hafter yer." And they did. "Git another cab, boys," said one of my protectresses; "hit's Miss Soldene, as sings hat th' 'Lambra, you know, 'Silver Threads hamong th' Gold.'" And they got another cabby, a sober one this time, and treated me with the greatest respect and consideration, all because I was an artiste and sang songs to the people.

And now, as we used to say in "Geneviève de Brabant," I have nearly come to "the end of our expedition." From July, 1892, to July, 1895, I resided in Sydney, New South Wales, whither I had been enticed by a business *ignis fatuus*, a Will-o'-th'-wisp—a Will-o'-th'-wisp, not of the most brilliant kind either. But no matter. When my futile Will-o'-th'-wisp disappeared in spluttering and splenetic incapacity, out of the darkness rose a gleam of light, which, gradually brightening, disclosed to my interrogative eyes a bottle of ink and a pen, a pen "pointing t'wards me." I seized the chance, also the pen, and for three years pursued the congenial occupation of pulling the beam from my cosmopolitan neighbour's eye, oblivious of the mote in mine own.

Returning to England after years of absence, one cannot but be astonished at the changes in theatres and music-halls, music-halls especially. Perhaps it will scarcely be credited when I say that on the vast Continent of Australia no such thing as a music-hall exists, not a music-hall as we used to understand it in the Oxford and Canterbury days, a music-hall with its little tables and chairs, a music-hall where a man took his sweetheart or his wife, where he heard some good music, a comic song, and smoked his cigar and drank his B. and S. No, they are all "variety theatres," and if the audience gets thirsty it goes out and has a drink at the contiguous bar. The same thing obtains in America. The only approach to an English music-hall I know of in the States is the Tivoli, in San Francisco, an opera house, open all the year round, admission and seat fifty cents (you can book them); where Offenbach and Sullivan, Wagner and Adams, Donizetti and Boito, Meyerbeer and Bizet, Gounod and Weber, Auber and Millocker, interpreted by artistes of respectable capacity, a good band and an excellent chorus, are successfully run in one continuous procession, from year's end to year's end, Sundays not excepted. Well, at the Tivoli, the audience can and do smoke till all is blue, and can and do have their drinks brought to them, and there they sit and sip, and the performance goes on amid soft murmurs of "Good," and "Bene," and "Bravo," and "Bis," for the Tivoli is comfortable and cosmopolitan. Travelling eastward through the States to England, I find on my arrival that the English music-hall has worked up to the "go-ahead" standard set by the American Variety theatre. In the States originated the practice of continuous turns—no wait, no dropping of curtains, simply a couple of flats drawn off (when I say "flats," I am not alluding to artistes, but to two pieces of scenery), or a "drop" taken up or down. The old day of the chairman's hammer and the drinks between the turns has disappeared, supplanted by an adaptation of transatlantic stage management that is undoubtedly effective.

Of course, no comparison can be instituted between the magnificence of the Empire, the Palace and the Alhambra of to-day, and the American Variety Show. The gorgeous, luxurious appointments of the English houses, the light, the gleam, the sparkle, and the gay *abandon* of the audience, the magnitude of the entertainment, and the ballet!—the ballet crowded with the most beautiful girls in the world, dressed in abbreviated costumes, designed by the finest artists of Europe, dancing to an immense band composed of splendid musicians, playing under the batons of eminent *chefs d'orchestre*.

They certainly have ballets in America, but they never look like the English ballet, because the costumes are always second-hand, imported after a year's wear in London; then the girls' shoes and tights are not properly looked after, and seventy-five per cent. of them don't know how to put their dresses on.

Then to complete the English *ensemble*, there are the world-renowned flunkeys, gorgeous in appearance, so gorgeous, that Li Hung, when at the Empire, took them for the directors; irreproachable in make-up and manners, indeed, so superlative in manners that sometimes a pin stuck suddenly into their silken-covered calves does not disturb their aristocratic and Vere de Vere calm.

Turning from these halls of dazzling light, one's mind turns back to those old times, and one cannot help wondering where the great respectable middle-class married music-hallist and his "Missus" have migrated to. Do they gravitate to the East-end, or do they no longer exist? Perhaps they have passed away with "Vilikins and his Dinah" and the "Ratcatcher's Daughter," or disappeared like the days of "Champagne Charley is me name," when people were satisfied with a magnificent orchestra of six, two out of the six being cornets.

So many people have asked me, "What made you think of writing?" Self-preservation was my first incentive, and when I got a chance of writing, I wrote. As a matter of fact, the first par. I perpetrated was an eloquent tribute to myself, and I am sure no one could have been more fully informed on the subject than I was.

But independent of this, I had nearly all my life been associated with writing people. When I was very young, but old enough to know better, I ran away and got married. My late husband was a son of Mr. Powell, the first sub-editor of the *Daily News* when it was founded in 1846, the chief being Mr. Charles Dickens.

Charles Dickens and my father-in-law were very old friends, and had been in the "gallery" together.

Mr. Powell, in his young days, lived in the York Road, Lambeth; next door to him lived Mr. George Hogarth, the eminent art and dramatic critic and writer. The girls and boys of the two families were always in and out the two houses. One day, Mr. Dickens, dining with Mr. Powell, met there Miss Catherine Hogarth, the future Mrs. Charles Dickens, and my subsequent connection with the Powell family explains how I crept into a sort of association with a literary circle.

And if these pages are (as I dare hope) found to be amusing in the slightest degree, why then I shall consider my intrusion justified, and in the words of the song will say to my reading public, not " Good-bye," but " Au revoir."

THE END.

INDEX.

A.

Abrahams, Mr. Morris, 91.
Adams, Annie, 51.
Adams, Miss, 12.
Addison, Mr. 90.
Aimée, Mme., 174.
Albani, Mme., 14.
Albertazzi, Mdlle., 58.
Alias, M., 92.
Ambrose, John, 43.
Anglesea, Marquis of, 140.
Appleby, George, 146.
Arditi, Mme., 24.
Arditi, Signor, 20.
Armitage, Sir George, 191.
Artot, Mme., 26.
Aston, Knight, 193.
Aston, Mrs., 197.
Auguste, Mrs., 141.

B.

Bailie, Mrs. Gordon, 198.
Ballantine, Sergeant, 123 *sq*.
Barber, Miss, 233.
Barnett, Morris, 280.
Barnum, Phineas T., 30, 242.
Barry, Helen, 120, 174.
Barry, Sheil, 231.
Bartleman, Mr. Tom, 34.
Bateman, Mr., 143.
Baylis, Ted, 43.
Beard, Harry, 43.
Belasco, Sam, 43.
Bellairs, Tom, 255.
Bellwood, Bessie, 260, 262.
Benedict, Jules, 40.
Benedict, Mr., 22.
Bennett, Sir John, 30.
Bertie, Miss, 233.
Beverly, E. D., 135, 144, 161.
Bishop, Alfred, 99.
Black, Colonel, 267.
Blandford, Marquis of, 140.
Bolt, Mr., 98.
Boston Brown, 130.
Boucicault, Dion, 68, 120, 161, 272 *sqq*.
Boucicault, Louise Thorndyke, 272.
Boucicault, Mrs. Dion, 271 *sq*.
Bracy, Mr. and Mrs., 219.
Braham, Mr. Augustus, 31.
Branscombe, Maud, 188.
Brayley, Teddy, 43.
Brett, Mr. Justice, 127.
Brian, Mr. and Mrs., 36.
Bromley, Nellie, 189.
Brooke, Una, 161.
Brown, Davie, 47.
Brown, Dr. Lennox,
Brown-Potter, Mrs., 263.
Buckstone, 93.
Burnett, Mr., 277.
Burton, Captain, 147.
Bury, M. Felix, 108, 232.
Bush, Charlie, 43, 135.

C.

Calcott, Mr., 96.
Calvert, Mr., 131.

Campbell, C., 193.
Carlton, Mr. W., 89.
Carthew, Laura, 160.
Caulfield, Johnny, jun., 34, 220.
Caulfield, Johnny, sen., 34.
Celli, Frank, 89.
Chaplin, Mr., 44.
Chart, Mrs. Nye, 258.
Chizzola, Carlo, 150, 159, 192, 201 *sqq.*, 222.
Clarkson, sen., Mr., 64.
Clarkson, Mrs., 65.
Claxton, Kate, 193, 195.
Clay, Ned, 191.
Cohen, Mr. Isaac, 91.
Colonna, Mme., 94.
Collins, Sam, 31.
Colomb, Capt. G. W., 28.
Cook, Aynesly, 58, 80, 232.
Cook, Tom, 43.
Coppin, Mr., 229.
Costa, (Sir) Michael, 20, 33.
Coveney, Miss Harriet, 17.
Cowell, Sam, 31.
Croswick, Mr., 217.
Crofton, Haidee, 188.
Crouch, Louie, 32.
Cumming, Sir Gordon, 236.
Curran, M.P., Mr., 206.
Cushman, Charlotte, 169, 254.
Cushman, Sisters, 254.

D.

DALEY, J., 44.
Dallas, Mr., 233.
Dalton, Mr., 193.
Daly, Augustin, 257.
Daniels, Mattie, 202.
Darley, Miss, 274.
D'Aubans and Wardes, The, 36.
Davenport, Dolly, 279.
Davenport, Fanny, 159.
Davidson, Mr. J. L., 25.
Davidson, Mrs., 25.
Debreux, Mdlle., 79.
Delle, Sedie, 21.
Desclauzes, Mme., 138.
Devine, Miss, 233.

Dhuleep Singh, Maharajah, 234.
Dickens, Charles, 307.
di Murska, Ilma, Mme., 22, 23.
Dolaro, Selina, 73, 108, 116, 134, 145, 187, 272.
Douglass, Mr., 58.
D'Oyly Carte, Mr., 90, 186, 242.
Downey, Mr., 103.
Dowty, A. D., 96.
Drew Dean, 34.
Dubois, Camille, 83, 229.
Duelin, Mme., 281.
Dunn, Dick, 43.
Dunning, Miss Alice, 35.
Dunraven, Lord, 122.
Dunsmore-Muir, Rev. Dr., 280.
Durant, Cissy, 198, 209, 222.

E.

EDINBURGH, Duke of, 228.
Egan, Pierce, 29.
Egerton, Henry, 103.
Emden, Mr., 282.
Ewell, Miss, 135.
Eyre, Sophie, 271.

F.

FARLEY, Edward, 201.
Farnie, H. B., 61, 67 *sq.*, 101, 107 *sqq.*, 135.
Farquhar, Gillie, 121.
Farquhar, Sir Horace, 121.
Farquharson, Sir James, 120, 140.
Farren, Nellie, 85.
Fischer, Minna, 223.
Fisk, James, 168.
Fisk, Stephen, 171.
FitzHenry, Miss, 18, 34, 38, 45.
Fleury, General, 122.
Foli, Signor, 46.
Forbes, Archibald, 241, 242.
Fortescue, Miss, 12.
Foster, Billy, 43.
Francis, Mr., 102.
French, Fred, 36.

G.

GAMBART, Mr., 30.
Garcia, Viadot, 21.
Gardiner, Mr., 216.
Gerard, Lady, 121.
Gerrish, Miss, 94.
Gibbons, C., 161.
Gideon, Johnny, 43, 92.
Gifford, Lord, 121.
Gillert, Mdlle., 234.
Gladstone, Rt. Hon. W. E., 251 *sqq.*
Glover, Mr. Howard, 10 *sqq.*
Glover, Mrs., 10 *sqq.*
Glover, William, 103.
Goddard, Mdme. Arabella, 25.
Goff, Mr., 34.
Gould, Jay, 199.
Grau, Maurice, 150, 159.
Green, Mr., 34, 36.
Greenwall, Harry, 181.
Gregory, Lady, 189.
Grey, Mabel, 52.
Grey, Marie, 29.
Grey, Miss Lennox, 81.
Grisi, Mme., 14, 21, 27.
Grossmith, George, 90.
Guerrabella, Mme., 14.
Guiglini, 21.
Gunn, John, 128.
Gunn, Michael, 187.
Gunniss, Misses, 34.
Gye, Mr., 20.

H.

HALTON, P. W., 96.
Hamp, "Tommy," 42.
Hanlon, Bros., 35.
Harbord, Purser, 153.
Harrington, Mrs., 130.
Harris, Augustus, 54, 58, 96, 137.
Harris, Charles, 256.
Harris, Mr. (Sir) Augustus, 236, 256.
Hastings, Marquis of, 44.
Hauk, Miss Minnie, 22.

Hawthorne, Nathaniel, 285.
Hay, Lord John, 121.
Haydon, 30.
Head, Mr. Charles, 43, 87, 105, 126, 134.
Hedderwick, Mr., 127.
Hengler, Mr., 70.
"Hermit," 44.
Hersee, Henry, 72, 247.
Hersee, Rose, 256.
Hertz, Dr. Cornelius, 199.
Hervé, M., 61, 65, 69 *sq.*, 98.
Hogarth, Catherine, 307.
Hogarth, Mr. George, 29, 307.
Hohler, Mr. Tom, 24.
Hollingshead, John, 50, 85, 98, 126, 135.
Holms, Mr., 147.
Honey, George, 96.
Hope, Lady Frances, 265.
Hopper, Mr. de Wolf, 265.
Horton, Priscilla, 130.
Hoskins, Henry, 6, 224.
Howard, Mr. J. B., 133.
Howard, Mrs. J. B., 12, 133.
Huddart, Mme. Fanny, 59.
Huddleston, Q.C., 122 *sq.*
Husk, Mr., 34.

I.

IRVING (Sir) Henry, 90, 130.

J.

JACOBI, M., 233.
Jamieson, —, 279.
Jarrett, 159.
Jefferson, Joe J., 279.
Johnson, Mrs., 31.
Johnston, J. B., 279.
Jolly, Mr., 144.
Jolly Nash, 35.
Jongmanns, Mr., 18, 33.

K.

KEAN, Mr. and Mrs. Charles, 281.

Keene, 199.
Keene, Laura, 275, 277.
Kelleher, Mr., 233.
Kendall, Mr. and Mrs., 100.
Kennedy, Capt., 150.
King, Katie, 36.
King, Tom, 43, 255.
Kiralfys, The, 35.

L

LANE, Mrs. Sarah, 93.
Langtry, Mrs., 231, 263.
Larkin, Captain Harry, 86.
Laurant, E. 161.
Laverne, Patty, 140, 187.
Lavine, Miss, 15.
Lawrence, Alberta, 31.
Lawson, Lionel, 138.
Lazaar, Sam, 212, 222.
Leader, Mr., 235.
Leblanc, Leonide, 86.
Leclerq, Lottie, 282.
Lee, General Robert, 175.
Lee, Miss Jennie, 81.
Lee, Rose, 232.
Lee, "Ted," 210.
Leeson, Dan, 277.
Le Fevre, Miss, 202.
Leggett, Mr., 103.
Leigh, Ada, 109.
Leigh, Mrs., 135.
Lely, Mr., 237.
Levey, W. C., 96, 123.
Lewens, Mr. H., 108, 160, 232.
Leybourne, George, 36.
Liddell, Maggie, 223.
Li Hung, 305.
Lindheim, M., 123.
Lingard, Mr. Horace, 35.
Litton, Marie, 275.
Lloyd, Arthur, 36.
Loseby, Constance, 220, 232.

Lutz, Meyer, 36, 136.
Lyndhurst, Agnes, 160.
Lyster, Mr. and Mrs. Saurin, 220.

M.

MAAS, Joseph, 120.
McAllister, Ward, 181.
McCaul, Col., 262.
McConnell, Mr., 100.
McCulloch, John, 198.
Macduff, Lord, 140.
Mackney, 31.
Maclagan, Tom, 36, 78.
Maitland, Mrs., 69.
Mallandaine, Mr., 98.
Manchester, Duke of, 240.
Mandeville, Lord, 260.
Manns, M. August, 14.
Mansell, Mr., 61.
Mapleson, Mr., 20, 31.
Marchisio, Sisters, 25.
Marini, Mrs., 235.
Mario, 21.
Marius, 75, 84, 120.
Marshall, Edward, 36, 108, 129, sq., 135, 161, 232, 244, 253.
Mathews, Julia, 54, 56 sq., 134.
Maynard, Jimmy, 43.
Mayo, Lord, 121.
Melling, Alice, 245.
Melling, Tom, 34, 246.
Mellon, Alfred, 9 sq.
Milano, 76, 85.
Milbanke, Ralph, 121.
Modjeska, Mme., 201.
Molique, Herr, 39.
Mongini, 21.
Moore, 139.
Moore, Maggie, 200.
Moore, Pony, 45 sqq.
Morgan, Laura, 82.
Morgan, Wilford, 58.

Index

Morton, Mr. William, 19.
Muir, Emily, 72.
Mum, Col., 98.
Munroe, Katie, 189, 256.
Musgrove, Frank, 76, 79.
Muybridge, Mr., 86.

N.

NAGLE, Mr., 235.
Nathan, Miss, 12.
Naudin, M., 25.
Neale, Dr., 153.
Neild, Dr., 219.
Nesbitt, Mrs., 12, 255.
Newcastle, Dowager Duchess of, 24.
Newcastle, Duke of, 190.
Nichols, Harry, 256.
Nichols, Miss, 161.
Nilsson, Christine, 22.
Norton, Charley, 108.
Norton, Chippy, 43.
Norton, Miss, 233.

O.

OATES, Alice, 193.
Ochiltree, Tom, 181.
Odell, Mr., 82.
Oliver, Patty, 255.
Oliver-Somers, 58.
Osbaldiston, Mr., 254.
O'Shea, Mrs., 297.
Oudin, Eugene, 264.

P.

PAGET, Lady Florence, 35.
Paget, Lord Alfred, 140, 257 *sqq*.
Paget, Miles, 203.
Palmer, 159.
Palmer, Minnie, 73.
Pancoast, Professor, 173.
Paque, M., 34.
Paradise, Kate, 188.
Parker, Louise, 264 *sqq*.

Parnell, Charles Stewart, 298.
Patti, Mme. Adelina, 9, 14. 21.
Patti, Carlotta, 22.
Paul, Mr. Howard, 54.
Payne, Fred, 58, 90.
Payne, Harry, 58, 90.
Payne, W. H., 58.
Peabody, George, 286.
Pearl, Cora, 32.
Peers, Mr. Tom, 98.
Pembroke, Lord, 202.
Penley, 189.
Pertoldi, Mme., 234.
Perugini, Signor, 264.
Phelps, 6.
Phillips, Bobby, 43.
Pitt, Emily, 99.
Plummer, John, 96.
Plumpton, Alfred, 34.
Plumpton, Mr. and Mrs., 219.
Price, Miss, 92.
Prince Consort, 283.
Prince Imperial, 141.
Popoff, Admiral, 233.
Posnos, The, 130.
Powell, Mr., 307.
Power, Lady, 229.
Power, Nellie, 35.

Q.

QUEEN, The, 277, 281 *sqq*., 301.
Quinton, Mr., 249.
Quinton, Mrs., 137, 244.

R.

RAE, J. B., 108, 160, 177, 232.
Randall, Harry, 36.
Reed, Mrs. German, 130.
Reichart, Herr, 39.
Richards, Harry, 36.
Richardson, George, 16.
Rignold, George, 162.
Riley, Mr. and Mrs., 36.
Rivers, Miss, 233.
Rivière, M., 50.
Robertson, Agnes, 277 *sqq*.

Robson, 31.
Robson, Lizzy, 160.
Robson, Stuart, 159, 174.
Rodney, Lord, 121.
Rogers, " Jimmy," 133.
Rogers, John, 179.
Rosa, Mme. Parepa, 169.
Rosa, Mdlle., 234.
Rosebery, Lord, 140.
Roselle, Amy, 174.
Ross, G. H., 120.
Rouse, John, 98, 108.
Russell, Henry, 33.
Russell, John, 54, 56.
Russell, Lilian, 264.
Russell, Lizzie, 59.
Russell, Miss, 31, 33, 45.
Russell, Mrs. Judge, 190.
Ryan, Desmond, 58.
Ryder, John, 48.
Rymill, Mr., 88.

S.

St. Aubyn, Mr., 34.
St. Clair, Miss E., 161.
St. John, Captain, 207.
St. John, Florence, 237.
St. Leonards, Lord, 121.
Sala, George Augustus, 30.
Santley, 9, 38.
Santley, Kate, 36, 190.
Sara, Mdlle., 35, 94, 120, 134, 188, 198.
Scott, Clement, 116.
Schneider, 189.
Schofield, Harry, 98.
Sheridan, Amy, 86.
Sherrington, Louie, 36.
Sherrington, Mme., 27.
Sims Reeves, 14, 38.

Stanhope, Wyndham, 83.
Stanley, H. M., 194.
Stanley, Mr. Fred, 127.
Stead, 36.
Stella, Rose, 189, 198, 209, 210, 222.
Stokes, Edward, 168.
Stoyle, " Jimmy," 58.
Straight, Sir Douglas, 140.
Strange, Frederick, 50, 55.
Stuart, Miss, 233.
Sudlow, Bessie, 159, 186.
Sullivan, Fred, 189.
Sutherland, Duke of, 190.
Sutton, Mr., 235.
Swift, Mr., 15.

T.

Tamberlik, 21.
Tasca, Mme. Charlotte, 34.
Taylor, J. G., 135.
Tempest, Marie, 256.
Temple, R., 135.
Tennant, Hector, 121.
Thompson, Augusta, 99.
Thompson, Lydia, 101.
Thorne, Charles, 174.
Tietjens, Mme., 21, 24, 26, 31.
Tivoli, Signor, 31.
Tom Thumb, Gen., 30.
Toole, J. L., 85, 90, 100.
Tracy, Hetty, 97.
Trebelli, 21.
Tremaine, Annie, 85.
Turpin, Miss, 32.
Tyrell, Miss Kitty, 33.

V.

Index

Vito, Miss, 233.
Vokes Family, 51.

W.

WALES, H.R.H. Prince of, 118, 141, 279, 299 *sqq.*
Wales, H.R.H. Princess of, 141.
Wall, Harry, 51.
Wallace, J., 193.
Wallace, Vincent, 72.
Wallack, Mr. James, 32, 159.
Wallscourt, Lord, 86.
Walmisley, 34.
Wanganheim, Gus, 209.
Ward, Ada, 207.
Ward, Miss Genevieve, 14.
Webb, Harry, 129 *sq.*
Weippert, 10, 219.

Weiss, Mr., 39.
Weiss, Mme., 39.
Wells, Mary, 277.
Wheatley, Charles, 277.
White, Miss, 94.
Whitehead, Miss, 52.
Wilford, Miss Lily, 94.
Williamson, C. J., Mr. and Mrs., 200.
Wilmot, C., 81.
Wilson, 31.
Wilson, Sir Craycroft, 224.
Wilson, " Lardy," 35, 63, 137.
Wilton, Miss Marie, 15.
Winder, Mr., 235.
Wood, Annie, 185.
Wood, Mrs. John, 254.
Woodhouse, " Johnny," 121.
Wombwell, Sir George, 121, 140.
Wright, Sarah, 94.